Guide to Civil War Artillery Projectiles

by Jack W. Melton, Jr., & Lawrence E. Pawl

Thomas Publications
Gettysburg, Pa. 17325

Additional titles by the authors:

Introduction to Field Artillery Ordnance 1861-1865
(Melton & Pawl, 1994)

Thomas Publications
3245 Fairfield Road
Gettysburg, PA 17325

The authors invite comments, corrections, and additional information from the readers. New information is most appreciated and will be acknowledged in future editions of this book. Correspondence and inquiries can be addressed to co-author Melton's attention at jack@jwmelton.com.

LIBRARY OF CONGRESS CATALOGING IN PUBLICATION DATA

Melton, Jack W., Jr., and Pawl, Lawrence E.
MELTON & PAWL'S GUIDE TO CIVIL WAR ARTILLERY PROJECTILES.

1. United States—Armed Forces—Ordnance and ordnance stores —History—19th century. 2. Artillery, Field and mountain—United States—History—19th century. 3. United States—History—Civil War, 1861-1865—Equipment and supplies.
#94-080240

ISBN-1-57747-106-7

Cover and interior photography by Jack W. Melton, Jr.

Title artwork by Joe Troxtel

Typography and design by Nancy Dearing Rossbacher
Fit To Print Desktop Publishing Services
Post Office Drawer 729, Orange, Virginia 22960

Dedication

The authors truly believe that without the extraordinary love and support from our families and special friends throughout the years of work it took us to complete our first book, *Introduction to Field Artillery Ordnance 1861-1865,* we would not have attempted to write this second book. We wish to thank each and every one of you for your patience with us while we were away from home on those long weekends and your understanding of why we needed to spend hundreds and hundreds of hours on the phone. Without your love our work would have been meaningless.

This book is dedicated to you.

Jack William Melton, Sr.   Lillian Pawl
Winona Love Melton   Brenda Vredeveld
Robert Troup Melton   Andrew Pawl
Caroline Melton Ferguson   Sarah Pawl

Acknowledgments

The authors sincerely appreciate the following individuals who graciously offered their knowledge and expertise, without which this work would not have been possible. We extend particular thanks to three individuals for their invaluable work on the initial draft of this book: Winona Melton, Henry Higgins, and Peter Jørgensen.

Paul Ackermann,
    West Point Military Academy Museum
Marsha Alexander
Howard Alligood
Alan C. Aimone, Chief Special Collections,
    United States Military Academy Library,
    West Point, New York
Kim Baker
Donald S. Ball
Barry Banks
Dr. Rick Beard, Atlanta History Center
William Dewey Beard
Glenn Beckham
Jack Bell
Jim W. Bell III
Dr. John Neal Brown
Kenneth P. Brugioni
Chris Bullington
Ronald E. Bupp
Kathy Bulson
Leroy Burgess
Brant Calvit
Michael Carpenter
Steve Chapin
Michael Cherry
Lawrence Christopher
Freddy Clark
William Cole, Eastern National
    Park & Monument Association,
    Gettysburg, Pennsylvania
Dennis Cox
Rex Cockerham
John Colgan
Greg Craven
Ray Davenport, Sumter Military Antiques
David Davidson
Warren Demarest
Bo Dubose, The Atlanta History Center
Lawrence H. Eckert, Jr.,
    Gettysburg National Military Park
Fred R. Edmunds, The Confederate
    States Armory & Museum
George Esker
Jerry Fertitta, The Richmond Arsenal
Edward Fisher
Robert W. Fisch, Curator of Arms,
    West Point Military Academy Museum
Jerry Foster
Tim Garrett, The Picket Post
N. Gibson Jr.
Mary Giles, Assistant Archivist,
    The Charleston Museum
Robert Glessner
Greg Griffin
Brenda Groenendyk
Kenneth Hamilton
Bob and Linda Hammonds
Charles S. Harris
Nick Harris

D. Scott Hartwig, Supervisory Park Ranger,
    Gettysburg National Military Park
Bill Henderson, The Picket Post
Larry Hicklen
Steve Hill
Samuel P. Higginbotham II
The Horse Soldier of Gettysburg:
    Sam, Wes, Chet, and Pat Small
Barry Hocutt
Thomas Holley
Gerald & Anna Hovater
Paul Hricz
Corky Huey
Mary A. Huff
Jerry Imperio
Robert Imperio
Jerry Jackson
Donald J. Jardine
Paul D. Johnson
Tammy Johnson
Chuck Jones
Gordon Jones, The Atlanta History Center
C. Peter and Kay Jørgensen,
    The Artilleryman magazine
Dennis Kelly, Kennesaw Mountain
    National Military Park
Mike Klinepeter
Lawrence Laboda
Thomas Laboda
Wendell W. Lang
Scott & Bev Launiere
Jeffrey Lea
Carole A. Lee
Lewis Leigh, Jr.
William Leigh
Steven E. Lister
Eugene Lomas
George H. Lomas
Dr. Francis Lord
Donald E. Lutz,
    Antique Ordnance Publishers
Michael J. McAfee, West Point
    Military Academy Museum
Joyce McDaniel,
    North South Trader's Civil War magazine
John Marcinkowski
Alan Marshal
Glen E. Mattox
Mike Meier, National Archives Archivist
Michael Milano
Steve E. Mullinax
Michael Musick, National Archives Archivist
R.E. Neville, Jr.
Michael J. O'Donnell
Edwin Olmstead
Gary Pass
H. Hume Parks
Bernard and Bruce Paulson,
    Paulson Brothers Ordnance Corp.

Steve Phillips
Mike Pilgram, National Archives Archivist
John & Karen Pizon
Denny Pizzini
Daniel V. Popham
Lee Poss
Russ A. Pritchard, Director, Civil War
    Library and Museum, Philadelphia
Stephen K. Quick
Patricia Quinn
Steve Ransbotham
Brian Reil
Andy Rice
Scott & Robin Riddle
Harry E. Ridgeway
Warren Ripley
Bruce Roberts
Peter Rockefeller
Nancy Dearing Rossbacher,
    North South Trader's Civil War magazine
    and Fit To Print Desktop Publishing
Betty Sanders
T. Scott Sanders
William R. Scaife
Wes Schiwitz
William S. Smedlund
Bill Smith
Stone Mountain Relics, Inc.:
    John Sexton, Lori Nash Cosgrove,
    Charles and Nan Nash
Carl Sitherwood
Frank Smith
Smithsonian Institute, Washington, D.C.
Steven J. Sollott
Wayne E. Stark
Steve W. Sylvia, Publisher's Press, Inc.,
    Publisher of *North South Trader's
    Civil War* magazine
Chris Taras
Dean S. Thomas, Thomas Publications
Joe & Kelly Troxtel
Linda Vander Lugt
Warren Vitellaro
Frank Warren
Ronnie Webb
Warren West, Jr.
Warren West, Sr.
Laura Westbrooks
Gary Wiggins
Peter Wilkerson, Archivist,
    South Carolina Historical Society
Gary Wilkinson
Donald Williams
Wayne Williams
Kenneth W. Williams
George F. Witham
F. Paul Wohlford
Earl Young

Preface

During the American Civil War, more varieties of projectiles and cannon were used than in any other time in military history. The outbreak of hostilities in 1861 found inventors on both sides searching for the perfect blend of sabot, shell body, and fuze to create the artillery projectile that would give the military advantage to their respective cannoneers. The vigorous pursuit of that elusive, perfect projectile continued until the end of the Civil War.

As a result of these seemingly endless innovations, the student of Civil War ordnance today faces a fascinating and potentially confusing maze of battlefield-tested artillery projectiles.

This volume has been written for the purpose of helping the reader better understand the varieties of ordnance used by the Confederate and Federal forces. This book is not intended, nor should it be used, as the absolute final word on this fascinating area of research. The authors have made every effort to be accurate, and whenever possible, archival and patent records have been used to support the information contained herein. Since our first book, *Introduction to Field Artillery Ordnance 1861-1865,* was published, continuing research by the authors as well as information provided by our readers has led to further understanding of this field. This new knowledge has been incorporated into this book. Historical research is an ongoing endeavor, and we invite the readers to share new information with us so that future editions will continue to be as accurate as possible.

Those readers who desire further detailed information will find a recommended reading list in the bibliography in Appendix B, page 91. An extensive glossary, provided to help the reader with technical artillery terminology, can be found in Appendix A, page 88.

An 1863 photograph of the devastating effects of a 32-pounder shell.

Table of Contents

I.   **Basic Facts Concerning Field Artillery**...8

II.   **An Inside Look at Field Artillery Projectiles**

     A.   Cross-sections of projectiles 9
     B.   How field artillery fuzes worked..............................20
     C.   Quick identification of fuzes 24

III.   **Field Artillery Projectiles: A Pictorial Study**

     A.   Combat Proven
         Spherical 29
         Canister
             Miscellaneous 35
             Hotchkiss 36
             Sawyer...37
             James 38
         Hot Shot, James 39
         Stand of Grape & Quilted Grape 40
         Archer 41
         Armstrong 48
         Blakely 49
         Britten 50
         Brooke 51
         Broun 52
         Dyer 53
         Hotchkiss 54
         James & James copies 58
         Mullane 61
         Read, Parrott & Read-Parrott 63
         Sawyer...75
         Schenkl & Schenkl copies 76
         Selma 79
         Whitworth & Whitworth copies 81

     B.   Post-War / Non-Combat Proven
         Absterdam 85
         Delafield 86
         Hotchkiss 87

IV.   **Appendixes**

     A.   Glossary 88
     B.   Bibliography 86
     C.   Index 92

I.

Basic Facts Concerning Field Artillery

The use of field artillery has always had a demoralizing effect on soldiers. Throughout the Civil War, the tactical use of field artillery evolved as the quality of field ordnance improved. Nothing was more frightening to the infantry of both sides than having to charge against emplacements of cannon firing shot, shell, and canister with devastating precision.

Experimentation led to diversity

Innovations in artillery development were slow to gain acceptance in the United States during the first half of the 19th century. Inventors spent years on experimentation, field trials, obtaining financial support, and engaging in the inevitable political maneuvering. All of this was necessary to have any newly developed artillery projectile or cannon reviewed by the Federal Ordnance Department for possible military approval.

Prior to the outbreak of hostilities in 1861, innovations in artillery were slow to gain acceptance; however, developments in the field of artillery reached a near fever pitch in both the Federal and Confederate war departments. Robert P. Parrott of Cold Spring, New York, and Dr. John B. Read of Tuscaloosa, Alabama, were the two preeminent pre-war pioneers in the design and production of rifled artillery projectiles and cannon. Read offered his services to the Confederacy, while Parrott remained loyal to the Federal government. These two inventors produced more artillery patterns and varieties of projectiles than any other inventors during that period.

Smoothbore cannon were manufactured with a smooth-sided bore that fired a spherical projectile (cannon ball) and/or conical canister. Rifled cannon were manufactured with spiral grooves designed to fire an elongated projectile. When fired, the elongated projectile's sabot entered these grooves, causing the projectile to spin around its own axis and thereby increasing range and accuracy.

All this activity led to rapid diversification in field artillery projectiles and cannon systems. One can imagine the problems encountered by an army that had to carry 2.9-inch, 3-inch, 3.67-inch, and 4.62-inch calibre projectiles for each of the different cannon systems in the field. Standardization of cannon calibre was desperately needed, but it was not until near the end of the war that the 3-inch rifle and 12-pounder smoothbore (4.62-inch calibre) cannon became the unofficial standards for field artillery use.

Rifled ordnance vs. smoothbore

The ordnance available early in the war was approximately one-third rifled, with smoothbore (6- and 12-pounder cannon) making up most of the remaining two-thirds. As of December 1, 1861, there were only 100 wrought-iron (ordnance) rifles and 193 Parrott rifles of both field sizes on hand, and only 36 Model 1857 12-pounder smoothbore Napoleon cannon for the Federal artillery. The rest of the Federal Army was equipped with Model 1841 6-pounders, heavy 12-pounders, and 12-pounder field howitzers—all smoothbores. Younger artillery officers were impressed with the rifled system; older, more experienced officers felt that the smoothbore cannon was equally important.

As the war progressed, many battles occurred at close range, under which condition the 12- pounder canister proved to be both deadly and defensive. The rifled artillery proved to be better for offense because of the accuracy and long range of its shell and case-shot projectiles.

The Confederacy & British imports

At the outbreak of hostilities in 1861, most of the ordnance and cannon the Confederates States had at its disposal were in the captured Federal armories and fortifications. Unfortunately, the quantities of ordnance were not great. Most accounts place the initial Confederate cannon cache at thirty-five field artillery pieces. This information is found to be inaccurate: it refers only to field artillery pieces and only the ones captured in forts taken over by the Confederates. Alabama alone seized approximately 100 cannon (24-and 32-pounders) in its seacoast forts on January 15, 1861, even before the state seceded.

Since initially the South only had one functional cannon foundry (Tredegar Iron Works in Richmond, Virginia) with which to supply its armies, outside sources were needed to meet demands. Great Britain was one of the many sources of projectiles and cannon used by the Confederacy. Of these British imports, the Whitworth system is the most recognized due to its unusual bore-shaped projectiles. Other British imports included the Armstrong, Britten, and Blakely systems of cannon and projectiles.

II. An Inside Look at Field Artillery Projectiles

A. Cross-sections of Projectiles

The projectiles in this section have been disarmed and cut in half by professionals using remote-control equipment. Under no circumstances should this be attempted by anyone without the proper training and equipment necessary to perform this life-threatening task safely. The authors do not encourage the reader to perform this work, nor do they hold themselves responsible for anyone attempting to do so. Special thanks go to Corky Huey and Andy Rice for their invaluable assistance in providing the Civil War hobbyist with this rare glimpse of the inner workings of artillery projectiles.

This section is intended to give the reader a better understanding of the construction, design, and purpose of Civil War field artillery projectiles. Various elements of the projectiles will be numbered and descriptions provided. In addition, the reader will be referred to other sections for more information. A review of the glossary section located in Appendix A, pages 88-90, would be helpful in understanding the terms used.

Index of half shells on the following pages

Spherical projectiles 10, 18
Dyer projectiles 12
Hotchkiss 13
James 14
Parrott 15
Read-Parrott and Read 16
Schenkl 17
Conical 19

> ### Do not attempt to defuse a shell yourself

Steve Phillips, a noted professional with over two decades of experience in disarming, states: "First and foremost, *do not* attempt to defuse a War Between The States shell. Unless you have positive proof that a shell has been properly unloaded, assume that it is live. These shells *can* explode. They will explode underwater and they will explode unexpectedly when being drilled. The only attitude to take when unloading shells is to assume that they are going to explode while drilling, whether underwater or not. The black powder inside a War Between The States projectile does not go bad inside the shell, and in some cases it is more potent today than when it was manufactured. Within the last ten years there have been at least six instances of shells exploding while being unloaded. The only way to unload a live shell is by remote rig, and this work should be left to others.

"Even shells that appear to have been unloaded can sometimes pose a threat if that unloading was done improperly. Air pockets are often present inside shells and these can cause damage similar to a powder explosion.

"There are collectors out there who know how to properly unload a shell, and you should contact them for this service. Don't risk your life and limbs over an old rusty piece of scrap iron. I honestly feel that due to people attempting to improperly unload a live shell, we have yet to see the last casualty of the war."

Above, Pvt. D.W.C. Arnold poses proudly for the camera.

Fig. II A-1
Confederate Spherical

Fig. II A-2
Confederate Spherical

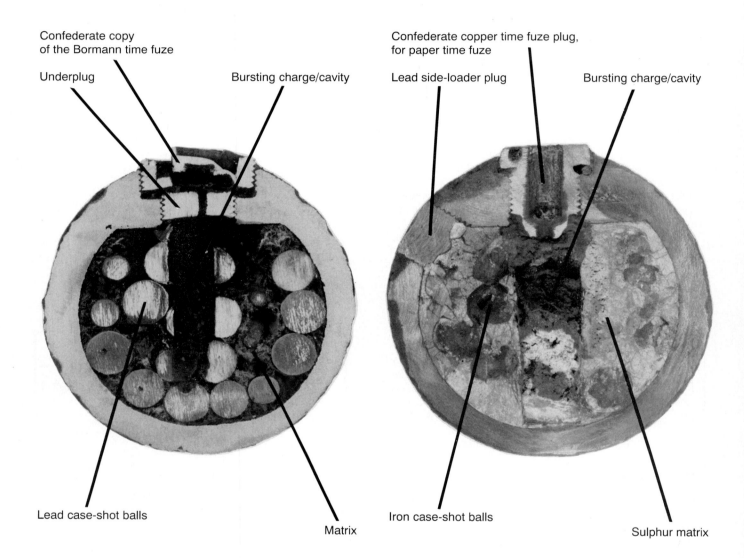

Confederate copy of the Bormann time fuze

Underplug

Bursting charge/cavity

Lead case-shot balls

Matrix

Confederate copper time fuze plug, for paper time fuze

Lead side-loader plug

Bursting charge/cavity

Iron case-shot balls

Sulphur matrix

In some cases the Federal spherical case-shot projectiles contained the bursting charge in a metal cylinder. The Confederates usually drilled into the case-shot to form the bursting charge cavity. Note the lead balls that were cut by the drill in Fig. II A-1. Due to the shortage of lead needed by the Confederates for small arms ammunition, iron case-shot balls were often substituted for lead, as can be seen in Fig. II A-2. This created a problem in that when the Confederates attempted to drill into the iron case-shot, the drill bit could not penetrate the hardened balls easily and would often bind, causing the matrix to break loose.

The process used to construct Fig. II A-2 is as follows: After the casting was removed from the mold, the fuze and side-loader holes were finished and threaded, a dowel was inserted into the fuze hole to the opposite side, and the iron balls were inserted through the side-loader hole, followed by hot matrix. After the matrix cooled the dowel was removed, leaving a space for the bursting charge. Compared to canister, case-shot projectiles had a greater effective range when used as an anti-personnel weapon.

Fig. II A-3
Confederate
Spherical

Fig. II A-4
Confederate
Spherical

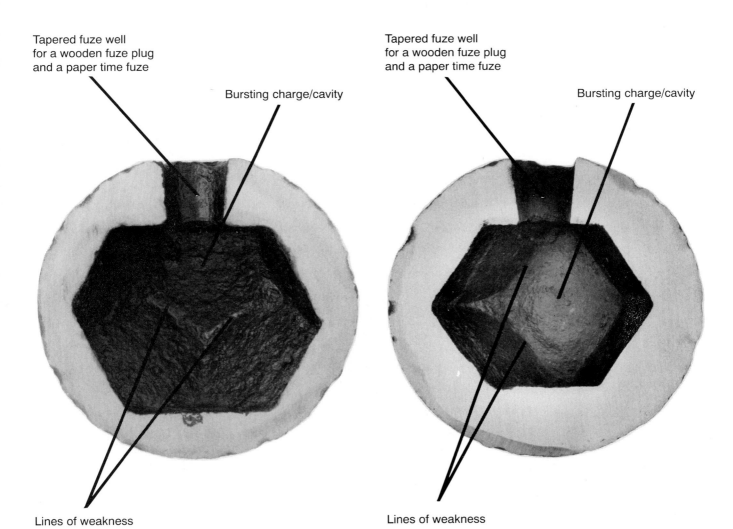

Tapered fuze well
for a wooden fuze plug
and a paper time fuze

Bursting charge/cavity

Tapered fuze well
for a wooden fuze plug
and a paper time fuze

Bursting charge/cavity

Lines of weakness

Lines of weakness

The concept of polygonal-cavity projectiles is generally attributed to Confederate Colonel John W. Mallet of Macon, Georgia, whose ideas may have been influenced by the segmented projectiles of British origin. There are at least four different designs of spherical projectiles with polygonal-cavity interiors known to the authors. The inner casting core created lines of weakness, which aided in the creation of a uniform number of fragments when ignition of the bursting charge fractured the projectile. This style of projectile was popular with the Confederate forces and was used extensively in the 1864 Atlanta Campaign in place of case shot. See page 30, figure III A-6, for a complete projectile.

Fig. II A-5
Federal, Dyer

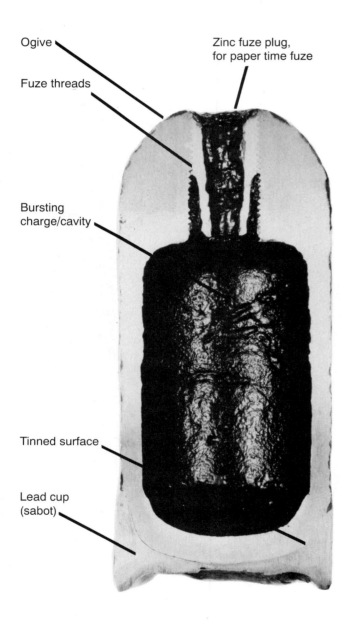

Ogive

Fuze threads

Zinc fuze plug, for paper time fuze

Bursting charge/cavity

Tinned surface

Lead cup (sabot)

This is an example of a Federal Dyer projectile. Located in the National Archives in Washington, D.C., and in *The War of the Rebellion (Official Records)* is information that supports the conclusion that the projectile is of Federal manufacture. Note the tinned surface between the iron base of the projectile and the lead cup (sabot). See page 53, figure III A-60, for further comments and a complete specimen.

Fig. II A-6
Federal Dyer

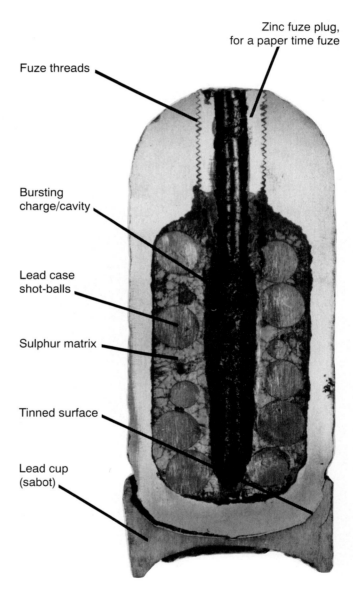

Fuze threads

Zinc fuze plug, for a paper time fuze

Bursting charge/cavity

Lead case shot-balls

Sulphur matrix

Tinned surface

Lead cup (sabot)

The Federal Dyer 3-inch calibre projectile was manufactured in both common shell and case-shot. The pictured case-shot Dyer projectile contains lead balls in a sulphur matrix, which is typical of the 3-inch calibre Dyer projectile. The Dyer projectile was not manufactured after 1862.

Fig. II A-7
Federal
Hotchkiss

Hotchkiss brass
percussion fuze:

Anvil cap

Nipple

Fuze body

Plunger/slider

Safety device

Nose

Bursting
charge/cavity

Lead band
(sabot)

Casting flaw

Base cup

Fig. II A-8
Federal,
Hotchkiss

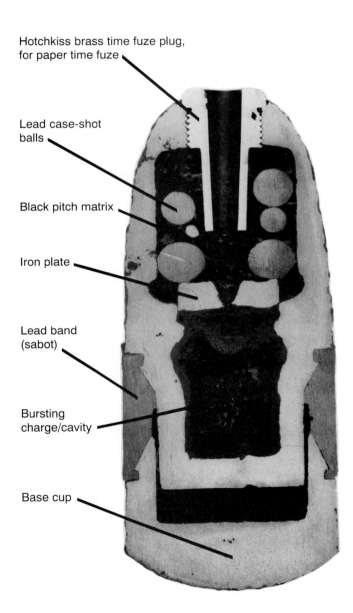

Hotchkiss brass time fuze plug,
for paper time fuze

Lead case-shot
balls

Black pitch matrix

Iron plate

Lead band
(sabot)

Bursting
charge/cavity

Base cup

The Hotchkiss pattern represented by Fig. II A-7 was designed to explode at the time of impact. It did not require flame grooves on the projectile body due to the percussion fuze system. This is an example of a projectile that does not contain case shot. Projectiles that contain only gunpowder in their bursting cavities are referred to as common shells. See page 55, figure III A-66, for a complete projectile.

This example is a case-shot variety of the Hotchkiss pattern. Hotchkiss patented on April 28, 1863, patent #38,359, an improvement employing an iron plate, to prevent the mixture of the case-shot balls and matrix with the bursting charge. This arrangement caused the case-shot to be thrown forward with greater velocity when the projectile detonated. See page 55, figure III A-65, for a complete specimen.

Fig. II A-9
Federal
James

Pattern I, Sub-pattern I

James percussion fuze:

Anvil cap (brass)

Nipple

Plunger/slider
(brass)

Powder train

Bursting
charge/cavity

Lead ring (sabot)

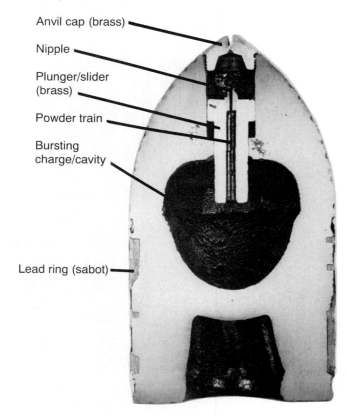

Fig. II A-10
Federal
James

Pattern II

James percussion fuze:

Anvil cap (brass)

Nipple

Plunger/slider
(brass)

Powder train

Bursting
charge/cavity

Lead ring (sabot)

Lathe dimple

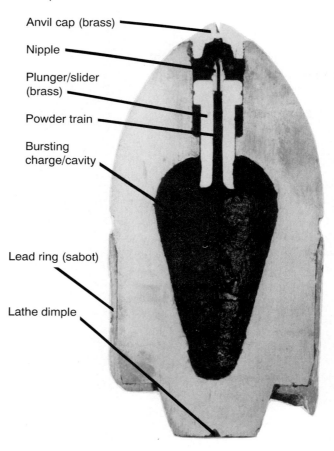

Charles T. James patented this projectile on February 26, 1856, United States patent #14,315. This James projectile is referred to as a James Pattern I, Sub-pattern I. See page 59, figure III A-79, for a complete example and additional comments.

Charles T. James patented this projectile on June 10, 1862, patent #35,521, as an improvement on his Pattern I. The specimen above is a James Pattern II projectile based on the date of the patent. In the field, the bursting cavity proved to be too small, resulting in poor fragmentation upon detonation. A large number of the James Pattern II projectiles have been recovered from the 1863 Siege of Vicksburg, Mississippi. See page 60, figure III A-79, for additional remarks and a complete specimen.

Fig. II A-11
Federal
Parrott

Fig. II A-12
Federal
Read-Parrott

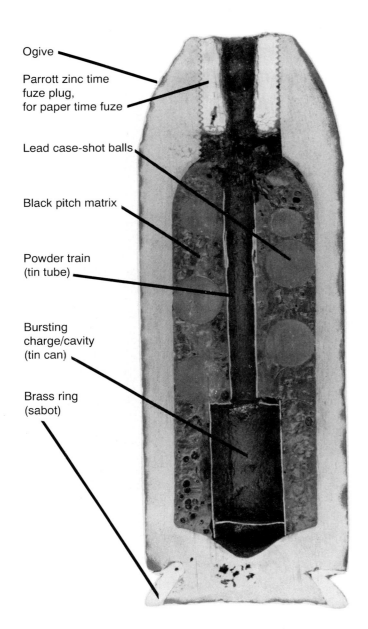

Ogive

Parrott zinc time
fuze plug,
for paper time fuze

Lead case-shot balls

Black pitch matrix

Powder train
(tin tube)

Bursting
charge/cavity
(tin can)

Brass ring
(sabot)

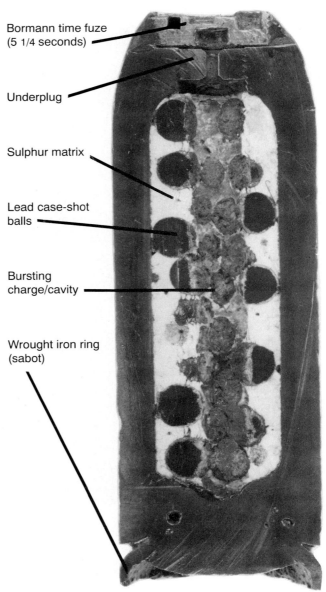

Bormann time fuze
(5 1/4 seconds)

Underplug

Sulphur matrix

Lead case-shot
balls

Bursting
charge/cavity

Wrought iron ring
(sabot)

Fig. II A-11 is a good example of the Federal Parrott case-shot projectile, which was manufactured in large quantities during the war. The black pitch matrix was patented by Alfred Berney of New Jersey on June 17, 1862, patent #35,659, and was an improvement over the sulphur matrix. In the manufacture of case-shot projectiles, Mr. Berney used in his matrix the residue from the distillation of coal-tar, generally known as "asphaltum." See page 65, figure III A-93, for a complete specimen.

The sulphur matrix used in the specimen above was often found to be brittle and therefore crumbled during formation of the cavity, unlike coal-tar, which was more flexible. Note that the bursting cavity was formed by drilling through the case-shot material. A Read-Parrott, 2.9-inch calibre projectile fitted with a Bormann time fuze is rare. The 5 1/4-second burning time of the standard Federal Bormann time fuze was insufficient for rifled artillery because its range was so much greater than that of smoothbore cannon.

Fig. II A-13
Confederate
Read-Parrott

Confederate copper time fuze plug,
for a paper time fuze

Bursting
charge/cavity

Bourrelet

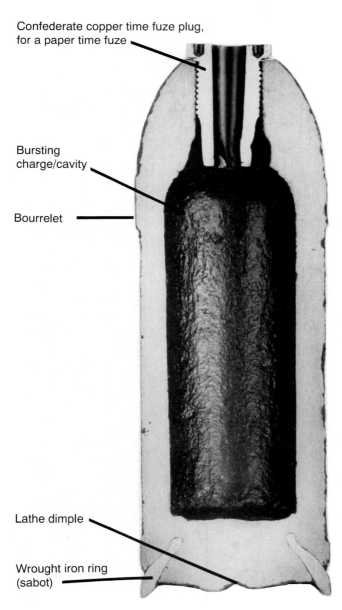

Lathe dimple

Wrought iron ring
(sabot)

Fig. II A-14
Confederate
Read

Confederate copper time fuze plug,
for a paper time fuze

Bursting
charge/cavity

Bourrelet

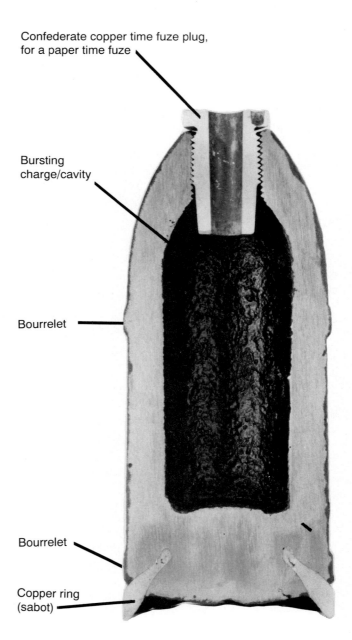

Bourrelet

Copper ring
(sabot)

The Read-Parrott above was most likely manufactured by Tredegar Iron Works in Richmond, Virginia. This is an example of a projectile that does not contain case-shot balls. Projectiles with this type of interior are often referred to as common shells. The term *common shell* refers to the interior construction and not the relative rarity of the projectile. See page 69, figure III A-102, for a complete specimen.

This is an example of the classic style of bourreleted Confederate Read projectile. The bourrelets were an attempt by the Confederates to save valuable time in the production and machining of projectiles. In manufacturing the Read projectile, the sabot ring (cup) of copper or brass was placed into a mold first and the iron forming the body added next. This resulted in the sabot being embedded in the cast iron body of the projectile. See page 72, figure III A-109, for a complete specimen.

Fig. II A-15
Federal
Schenkl

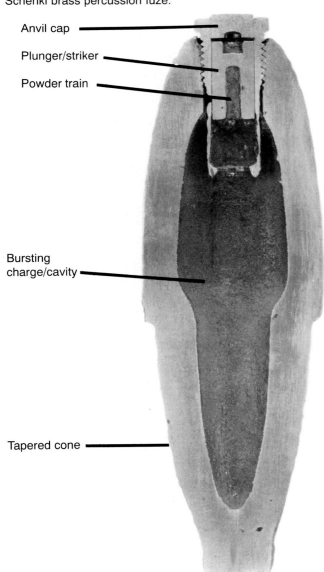

Schenkl brass percussion fuze:

Anvil cap

Plunger/striker

Powder train

Bursting
charge/cavity

Tapered cone

The common shell interior construction has a bursting charge cavity that does not contain case-shot material. This is an example of the most common Federal 3-inch Schenkl projectile manufactured. According to Abbot's *Siege Artillery in the Campaigns Against Richmond*, the Schenkl brass percussion fuze was 82% effective. Over 125,000 3-inch Schenkl shells were purchased by the Federal Ordnance Department. See page 76, figure III A-120, for a complete specimen.

Fig. II A-16
Federal
Schenkl

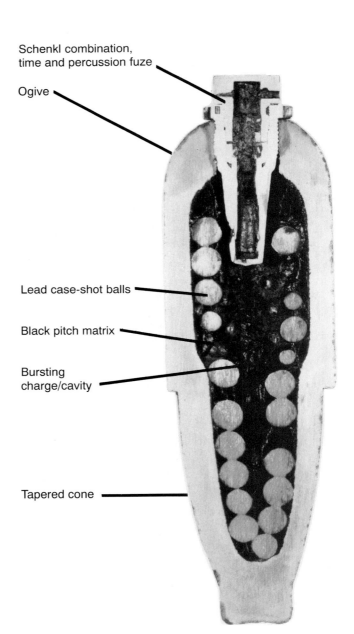

Schenkl combination,
time and percussion fuze

Ogive

Lead case-shot balls

Black pitch matrix

Bursting
charge/cavity

Tapered cone

The more rounded nose on this Schenkl projectile indicates that it contains case-shot. The 3-inch Schenkl case-shot projectile has only been recovered with lead case-shot balls and black pitch matrix. The Schenkl combination fuze was unreliable and under combat conditions was only 55% effective. Over 53,000 3-inch Schenkl case-shot projectiles were purchased by the Federal Ordnance Department. See page 76, figure III A-121, for additional remarks and a complete specimen. See page 22 for information about the fuze.

Fig. II A-17
Confederate
Spherical

Fig. II A-18
Federal
Read-Parrott

This is an example of a Confederate 12-pounder (4.62-inch calibre) spherical projectile with a polygonal-cavity interior. It was found exploded in the ground, recovered, cleaned, and reassembled. The lines of weakness are clearly evident in the equal-shaped fragments.

This specimen is an example of a Federal 10-pounder (2.9-inch calibre) Read-Parrott projectile. Like the specimen at left, it was found exploded in the ground and reassembled. Note that the projectile burst into random size fragments. No two artillery projectiles ever fragmented in a similar pattern unless they possessed a polygonal-cavity interior.

Fig. II A-19
Federal & Confederate
Conical

Fig. II A-20
Federal
Conical

Top iron plate

Iron canister balls

Top iron plate

Tin sides

Solder seam

Wooden sabot

Base iron plate

This specimen was reconstructed to illustrate the interior view of a standard 12-pounder (4.62-inch calibre) canister. Sawdust filled the spaces between the iron balls found in the pictured specimen. The tin sides are missing, as is the wooden sabot. Note that the top plate is thinner than the bottom plate, which had to absorb the initial discharge force during firing. This pattern of construction is typical of both Federal and Confederate canisters.

This non-excavated specimen is an example of the classic-style canister that both the Federal and Confederate forces used in the 12-pounder smoothbore cannon. The tin cylinder was dipped into a lacquer of beeswax dissolved in spirits of turpentine to prevent it from rusting. Canister was designed to be fired at close range with a resulting devastating effect on the enemy. It contained rows of iron balls packed with dry, sifted sawdust.

II. Field Artillery Projectiles

B. How field artillery fuzes worked

Civil War artillery fuzes, just like the projectiles, came in many different sizes, shapes, and varieties. While the primary purpose of the fuze was to explode the projectile among enemy forces, the methods used to accomplish this objective varied. In many cases, the artillerist was the one who decided what type of fuzing system to employ based on the range of the target, type of target, and type of projectile he intended to use. In other cases, the artillerist made the choice of projectiles and had to use the fuzing system manufactured into the projectile.

All fuzing systems can be broken down into four categories:

Time Fuzes
This system, the most commonly employed, was designed to explode a projectile after a pre-determined number of seconds. Two basic systems of time fuze were used. The first system was simply a powder composition, wrapped tightly in paper and pre-cut at the factory to determine the time before explosion. It was driven into a metal or wood fuze plug mounted in the fuze hole of the projectile. The second system employed a soft metal housing containing a powder train. The artillerist cut through the powder train at the appropriate time mark before loading the projectile into the cannon.

Both time fuze systems relied on the flame from the exploding powder charge in the cannon tube to ignite the powder composition. After the composition had burned down through the set number of seconds, the fuze flame would enter the powder chamber inside the projectile and cause the projectile to explode.

The most common projectiles found that employed the time fuze system are Parrott, Hotchkiss, and Bormann-fuzed spherical shells.

Percussion Fuzes
Percussion was the second most commonly employed fuze system. These were designed to explode the projectile when the fuze made contact with an object. Most percussion fuzes employed a plunger-and-anvil method of detonation. The fuze body was usually brass, copper, or alloy, and was threaded to be screwed into the nose of the projectile. When the fuze struck an object, a striker was driven down a chamber inside the fuze, where it struck a percussion cap (which was seated on a nipple) against the anvil. Employing the same principle as a musket, the percussion cap then exploded, sending a small flame through a hole in the nipple and igniting a powder train. The powder train transferred the flame to the powder chamber and detonated the projectile.

The common projectiles that employed the percussion fuze system are Parrott, Hotchkiss, James, and Schenkl.

Combination Fuzes
As the name implies, this system was a combination of the time fuze and percussion fuze systems. Combination fuzes varied widely in their method of detonation depending upon the inventor and manufacturer. The basic premise was that the fuze was set, prior to firing, to a specific detonation time. When the projectile was fired from the cannon tube, the shock (or inertia) of the firing caused a plunger to slide down and strike a chemical composition against a metal platform, causing a flame to ignite the powder train. If the projectile struck an object before the time element was completed, the system was designed to activate as a percussion fuze.

Combination fuze systems can be found on Armstrong, Schenkl, and Sawyer projectiles, among others.

Concussion Fuzes
These fuzes were designed to activate from the shock of striking an object. Once again, the actual mechanics of the fuze system varied according to the manufacturer and inventor. Some systems employed chemical vials which, when shattered upon impact, caused a fire that was transferred from inside the fuze body to the powder chamber. Other systems relied upon plaster to separate the igniting material from the powder until the plaster shattered upon impact. WARNING: Chemical concussion fuzes, especially the Tice concussion fuze, should be avoided by collectors unless it is known beyond any doubt that the vials have already been destroyed.

Many projectiles found in the field still retain their fuzing system. There are many reasons for the failure of a fuze system to detonate, but the most common explanations are that the fuze was damaged while being set into the projectile (by either the manufacturer or the artillerist), the fuze was damaged upon impact, or, as in the case of a percussion system, the projectile tumbled as it traveled and landed without the fuze striking anything. The examination of many projectiles recovered from battlefields revealed that the fuze worked properly but the projectile was defective in some way.

The fuze illustrations that follow are not meant to be inclusive or comprehensive with respect to all classes and examples, but rather to give the reader an overview.

Bormann Time Fuze

Fig. II B-1
Federal 5 1/4-second
Bormann time fuze

Fig. II B-2
Confederate 5 1/2-second copy
of the Bormann time fuze

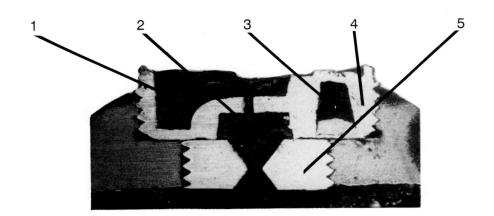

Fig. II B-3
Cross-section of the
Bormann time fuze

The Bormann fuze is named after its inventor, Belgian Army Captain Charles G. Bormann. The Bormann time fuze was employed by the United States Ordnance Department as early as 1852. The time fuze is contained in a tin and lead disk (4). This disk has time markings indicated in seconds and quarter-seconds graduated up to 5 1/4 seconds. The artillerist used a metal punch to pierce the thin metal at the desired time marking. This exposed a section in the horseshoe-shaped horizontal mealed powder train (3), which is covered by a thin sheet of tin. When the cannon discharged, the flame from the explosion ignited this powder train. It would burn in a uniform rate in both directions, but one end would terminate in a dead-end just beyond the 5 1/4-second mark (Confederate copies are 5 1/2 seconds). The other end would continue to burn past the zero-mark, where it would travel through a channel (1) to a small powder booster or magazine (2). This powder then exploded, sending the flame through a hole in the fuze underplug (5) to the powder chamber of the projectile. The purpose of the brass or iron fuze underplug was to form a solid base of support for the soft metal fuze, which could have easily been damaged during firing.

Schenkl Combination Fuze

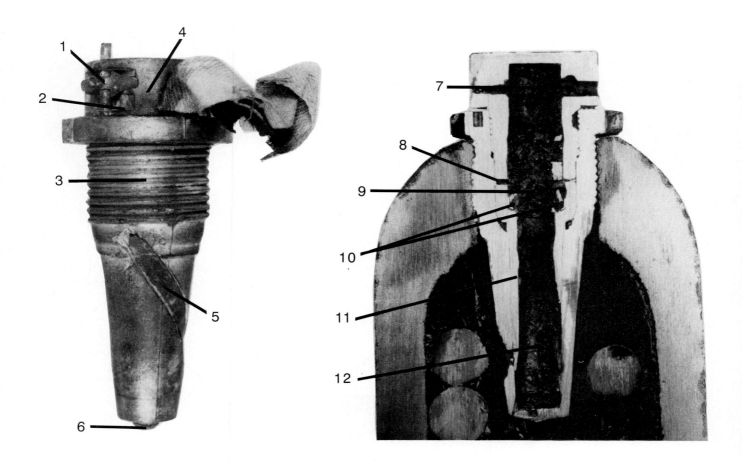

Fig. II B-4

Complete Schenkl Combination fuze

Fig. II B-5

Cross-section of the Schenkl Combination fuze

This fuze stock (3) is made of zinc and has a time index (2) on the face of the top flange graduated from zero to 9 1/2 seconds. The fuze body is closed at the bottom (6) and pierced by a series of small holes (5) spiraling down from the middle of the fuze body to the end. The rest of the fuze consisted of a combustible fuze compound (12) contained in a metal case which also had holes spiralling down but in an opposite direction from the body. A rotator (4) is screwed into the top of the fuze. Inside the rotator is the plunger, which is held in place by a soft metal pin and an iron safety pin. An interior fuze rotator (11), affixed to the top rotator by two metal dowels, contains a fulminate ring (10) and a highly combustible soluble cotton compound (9). When the artillerist was ready to arm the fuze, he removed the safety pin (placed where #7 points; pin is missing from this cutaway) and lifted the spring clip (1), set the rotator to the correct time (using a stamped arrow as a guide), and then locked the rotator in place. By doing this the two sets of holes lined up with each other to produce the proper burning time. The inertia of the cannon firing caused the safety pin (placed where #8 points; pin is missing from this cutaway) to break and threw the plunger back against the ring. The flame from that action caused the cotton to flare up and light the time fuze compound. The flame burned through the two holes into the projectile's powder chamber. If the projectile struck anything before the time fuze was through burning, the fuze body would break, causing the burning compound to drop immediately into the powder chamber.

Hotchkiss Time Fuze

Fig. II B-6

Complete brass Hotchkiss time fuze plug

Fig. II B-7

Cross-section of the brass Hotchkiss time fuze plug

This Hotchkiss fuze plug is made of brass and has a screwdriver slot across the face. The plug is threaded and was screwed into the fuze well of the projectile. A paper time fuze, composed of a powder composition tightly wrapped in paper, was then driven into the center of the plug. The length of the fuze determined the amount of time it took to finish burning. The artillerist could either choose a manufactured fuze or alter the length of a fuze so that it would burn for a shorter period of time. When the fuze burned through to the end, the flame was transmitted through the hole in the fuze plug and into the powder chamber of the projectile. This is a representative example of this class of time fuzes.

Parrott Percussion Fuze

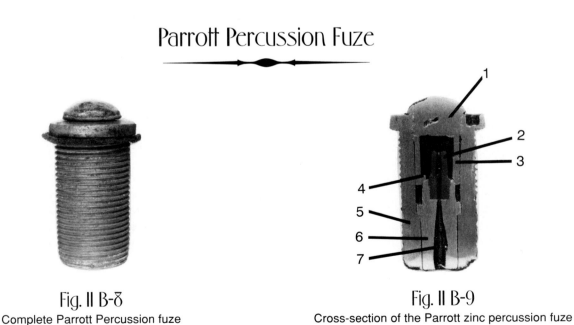

Fig. II B-8

Complete Parrott Percussion fuze

Fig. II B-9

Cross-section of the Parrott zinc percussion fuze

This type of Parrott percussion fuze saw extensive use. The fuze body (5) is made of zinc and was screwed into the fuze hole by a spanner wrench using the two spanner holes at the top of the fuze. An anvil (1) is screwed into the top center of the fuze. The interior contains a percussion cap (placed where 2 points; missing from this cutaway) seated on a nipple, the plunger or striker (6), and the powder train (7). The striker is held back by two small projections (4) on a safety pin (3). When the fuze impacted, the two projections broke and allowed the striker to move forward. The percussion cap struck the anvil and exploded, sending a flame through the nipple to the powder train. The flame was then transferred to the powder chamber of the projectile. This is a representative example of the class of percussion fuzes.

II.

Field Artillery Projectiles

C. Quick identification of fuzes

On the following two pages are numbered examples of selected artillery projectile fuzes. The numbers correspond to the following fuzes. The reader may also refer to the page and figure numbers shown for complete specimens containing the fuze.

(1) Packet of five 10 second paper time fuzes from Frankford Arsenal
(2) Packet of five 10 second paper time fuzes
(3) Arrick "Eureka" time fuze, brass
(4) Absterdam percussion fuze, brass
(5) Britten percussion fuze, brass   (page 50, figure III A-52)
(6) Britten percussion fuze for Blakely, brass   (page 49, figure III A-49)
(7) Parrott Type I percussion fuze, zinc   (page 65, figure III A-91)
(8) Parrott Type II percussion fuze
(9) Schenkl percussion fuze, brass   (page 76, figure III A-120)
(10) Schenkl percussion fuze, zinc   (page 76, figure III A-121)
(11) Sawyer percussion fuze, brass   (page 75, figure III A-119)
(12) Sawyer combination fuze, brass   (page 75, figure III A-118)
(13) Confederate West Point Type percussion fuze   (page 73, figure III A-113)
(14) James two-piece percussion fuze, brass   (page 59, figure III A-75)
(15) Hotchkiss percussion fuze, iron anvil cap   (page 57, figure III A-70)
(16) Paper time fuze
(17) Confederate copy of the Bormann time fuze   (page 31, figure III A-7)
(18) Underplug for Bormann time fuze   (page 10, figure II A-1)
(19) Federal Bormann time fuze   (page 32, figure III A-10)
(20) Britten time fuze, brass
(21) Absterdam time fuze, brass   (page 85, figure III B-3)
(22) Taylor time fuze
(23) Confederate replacement for the Bormann time fuze, copper   (page 34, figure III A-17)
(24) Confederate spherical projectile time fuze, copper   (page 34, figure III A-18)
(25) Confederate elongated projectile time fuze, copper   (page 69, figure III A-102)
(26) Confederate elongated case-shot projectile time fuze, copper   (page 70, figure III A-103)
(27) Brooke time fuze, copper   (page 51, figure III A-55)
(28) Wooden time fuze plug for rifled projectiles   (page 68, figure III A-99)
(29) Wooden time fuze plug for spherical projectiles   (page 30, figure III A-6)
(30) Confederate screwdriver slotted time fuze plug
    for spherical projectiles, brass   (page 30, figure III A-4)
(31) Hotchkiss time fuze, brass   (page 55, figure III A-65)
(32) Hotchkiss time fuze for case-shot, brass
(33) Hotchkiss time fuze for case-shot, lead   (page 55, figure III A-64)
(34) Hotchkiss time fuze for case-shot, brass   (page 57, figure III A-69)
(35) Parrott time fuze, zinc
(36) Parrott time fuze, zinc   (page 65, figure III A-93)
(37) Parrott time fuze, zinc   (page 66, figure III A-95)

1

2

3

4

5

6

7

8

9

10

11

12

13

14

15

16

17

19

20

21

22

18

23

24

25

26

27

28

29

30

31

32

33

34

35

36

37

The 17,000-pound weight of this mortar—known as "Dictator"— required that it be mounted on a railroad car strengthened with additional beams and iron plating. Federal artillerymen stand beside it in this photograph, taken near Petersburg in 1864.

Federals stand at attention at a fort near Atlanta in 1864.

III. Field Artillery Projectiles
A Pictorial Study

A. Combat proven

The following pictorial guide has been designed to be of maximum benefit to the beginning collector as well as the more advanced student. Each page is designed to serve as a quick reference guide for the most common varieties of artillery projectiles. With careful review, the reader will find valuable information to help point out many of the more subtle differences between apparently similar projectiles.

The comments located at the bottom of the each page deserve special attention. In addition to providing information concerning the projectiles illustrated, they may also refer the reader to other sections of the book to help clarify a point or to expand on a particular thought. Additional technical information can be found in the glossary located in Appendix A, pages 88-90.

In an attempt to keep collectors from getting confused when reading other reference material on projectiles, the authors have decided to continue referring to various patterns by their currently accepted common name. In the subtitles of and the technical information about some projectiles is a new term that the authors feel more precisely describes the inner construction of artillery projectiles. As defined by the authors, *construction* is a term describing the interior design of the projectile. Examples are solid shot, common shell, and case-shot.

In order to begin establishing standards in the artillery projectile field, a designation of the particular pattern, sub-pattern, or variant has been established. The authors have noted that in all previous books on artillery—including our first book, *Introduction to Field Artillery Ordnance 1861-1865*—there was no consistent method used in attempting to classify projectiles. Therefore, the authors have created a logical system based on patent dates whenever possible. When patent information was not available, the authors elected to use a classification based on the earliest known field use.

As with any first effort of this nature, revisions will be needed in this system of projectile classification. The authors look forward to comments and suggestions from fellow artillery enthusiasts.

Pattern	This is the most significant classification and is primarily based on the date of the patent or, if patent date is unavailable, the first known field use. In most cases the designations of pattern follow a chronological order of development in that particular style of projectile. Minor variations in body style, sabot, and fuzing systems do not affect the pattern designation.

Sub-pattern	Within a specific projectile pattern there can exist several significant variations in the body, sabot, or fuzing, and/or any combinations of the above. These are commonly referred to as sub-patterns. Example: the James Pattern I, Sub-pattern II projectile commonly called a tie-ring James. See page 59, figure III A-76 for an example.

Variant	Within a specific projectile pattern or sub-pattern there can exist minor differences, such as a wooden drive-in paper time fuze adapter and a threaded paper time fuze adapter. Projectiles with these minor differences are considered variants.

Fig. III A-1
Confederate Spherical

Fig. III A-2
Federal Spherical

Fig. III A-3
Confederate Spherical

DIAMETER:	3.57 inches
GUN:	6-pounder smoothbore, 3.67-inch calibre
LENGTH:	—
WEIGHT:	6 pounds 5 ounces
CONSTRUCTION:	Solid shot
SABOT:	Wooden cup (missing)
FUZING:	None

This was the most common 6-pounder (3.67-inch calibre) smoothbore projectile used by both Federal and Confederate forces. According to Gibbon's *The Artillerist's Manual*, "a 6- or 12-pound ball will go through six men at 800 yards' distance." Gibbon also states that "solid shot is of very little effect upon earthen parapets, unless it passes through, in which case it soon knocks them down. At 600 yards, shot from field-guns will penetrate from 5 to 6 1/2 feet into newly thrown-up earth."

DIAMETER:	4.50 inches
GUN:	12-pounder smoothbore, 4.62-inch calibre
LENGTH:	5 1/8 inches including sabot
WEIGHT:	12 pounds 5 ounces
CONSTRUCTION:	Solid shot
SABOT:	Wooden cup
FUZING:	None

The projectile above is non-excavated and rests on its original wooden sabot. This was the most common solid-shot projectile of any calibre used during the Civil War by both the Federal and Confederate forces. The ball is secured to the sabot by two crossed iron straps nailed to the wooden cup. The cartridge bag or powder bag was tied to the groove cut into the base of the sabot. After attachment of the powder charge, the round was referred to as fixed ammunition. The 12-pounder Napoleon smoothbore cannon firing a 12-pound solid shot with 2.5 pounds of service charge at a 5º elevation had a range of 1,680 yards.

DIAMETER:	5.63 inches
GUN:	24-pounder smoothbore, 5.82-inch calibre
LENGTH:	—
WEIGHT:	24 pounds
CONSTRUCTION:	Solid shot
SABOT:	Wooden cup (missing)
FUZING:	None

Solid-shot projectiles were designed for the purpose of destroying fortifications, cannon emplacements, trenches, and buildings. When fired on hard, dry ground it often ricocheted from one target to another. According to *The Confederate Field Manual*, "The initial velocity of a cannon ball is about 1,500 feet per second. It varies from 1,400 feet to 1,800 feet, depending on the weight of the charge and the strength of the powder."

Fig. III A-4
Confederate Spherical

Fig. III A-5
Confederate Spherical

Fig. III A-6
Confederate Spherical

DIAMETER:	3.57 inches
GUN:	6-pounder smoothbore, 3.67-inch calibre
LENGTH:	—
WEIGHT:	4 pounds 15 ounces
CONSTRUCTION:	Shell, polygonal cavity
SABOT:	Wooden cup (missing)
FUZING:	Confederate brass fuze plug, paper time fuze

Note the letter "G" stamped near the Confederate slotted brass fuze plug. This letter "G" is believed to indicate the site of manufacture of this projectile to be Selma Arsenal, Alabama. The interior construction of this particular shell is in the form of cast-in-lines of weakness and is commonly referred to as a polygonal cavity projectile. This type of construction is only found in Confederate-manufactured ordnance.

DIAMETER:	3.55 inches
GUN:	6-pounder smoothbore
LENGTH:	4 1/8 including sabot
WEIGHT:	3 pounds 6 ounces
CONSTRUCTION:	Shell
SABOT:	Wooden cup
FUZING:	Wooden fuze plug, paper time fuze

The specimen above is non-excavated and rests on its original wooden sabot. The ball is fixed to the sabot by a ring or collar around the fuze opening and secured to the sabot with four tin straps nailed to the wooden cup. Note the crude mold seam around the ball, typical of Confederate-manufactured projectiles. Note also the deep groove at the base of the wooden sabot, where the cartridge bag was tied in place.

DIAMETER:	4.49 inches
GUN:	12-pounder smoothbore, 4.62-inch calibre
LENGTH:	—
WEIGHT:	9 pounds 7 ounces
CONSTRUCTION:	Shell, polygonal cavity
SABOT:	Wooden cup(missing)
FUZING:	Wooden fuze plug, paper time fuze

Commonly called a polygonal-cavity projectile, this shell was used exclusively by the Confederates. The interior was cast with lines of weakness in the form of pentagonal sections so that it fragmented into twelve equal pieces. It is also found in diamond and trapezoid patterns. Note the "G" stamped to the left of the fuze plug, thought to signify manufacture at the Selma Arsenal in Alabama. The packing tow, still inserted in the fuze plug, protected the powder charge from foreign matter until it was removed prior to the insertion of the paper time fuze. See page 11, figure II A-3, for a cross-section.

Fig. III A-7
Confederate Spherical

Fig. III A-8
Federal Spherical

Fig. III A-9
Confederate Spherical

DIAMETER:	3.56 inches
GUN:	6-pounder smooth-bore, 3.67-inch calibre
LENGTH:	—
WEIGHT:	5 pounds 7 ounces
CONSTRUCTION:	Shell
SABOT:	Wooden cup (missing)
FUZING:	Confederate copy of the Bormann time fuze

This is a Confederate copy of the Federal-manufactured Bormann fuze and projectile. The Federals used this pattern until the 6-pounder smoothbore cannon was removed from the field in 1864. One indicator of Confederate manufacture is that the first line on the fuze is the full width of the powder train; the Federal Bormann fuze has a first line that is half the width of the powder train. Another is that the Federal Bormann fuze was only 5 1/4 seconds; the Confederate copy was 5 1/2 seconds. The Confederates discontinued their Bormann time fuze by 1863 due to difficulties in manufacturing and poor performance. See page 21 for the Bormann fuze.

DIAMETER:	4.50 inches
GUN:	12-pounder smooth-bore, 4.62-inch calibre
LENGTH:	4 15/16 inches w/sabot
WEIGHT:	8 pounds 7 ounces (if case-shot, 11-12 pounds)
CONSTRUCTION:	Shell
SABOT:	Wooden cup
FUZING:	Bormann time fuze

This shell is non-excavated and rests on its original wooden sabot. The wooden sabot was designed to align the fuze and keep it forward and centered in the cannon bore. The cartridge bag was tied in the deep groove cut into the base of the sabot. Twine was used to tighten down the four tin straps, holding the sabot and fuze collar more secure. The 12-pounder (4.62-inch calibre) projectile was the most common Federal shell employing the Bormann time fuze.

DIAMETER:	5.67 inches
GUN:	24-pounder smooth-bore, 5.82-inch calibre
LENGTH:	Approx. 7 1/4 inches w/sabot
WEIGHT:	20 pounds 3 ounces
CONSTRUCTION:	Shell
SABOT:	Wooden cup
FUZING:	Confederate copy of the Bormann time fuze

Note the well-preserved condition of the original wooden sabot and tin strapping, which can be seen nailed to the sabot. This particular sabot was manufactured by the Confederates without a cartridge bag groove. This specimen was recovered from the Savannah River near the site of the Augusta Powder Works, Augusta, Georgia.

Fig. III A-10
Federal
Spherical

Fig. III A-11
Confederate
Spherical

Fig. III A-12
Federal
Spherical

DIAMETER:	4.52 inches
GUN:	12-pounder smooth-bore, 4.62-inch calibre
LENGTH:	—
WEIGHT:	9 pounds 4 ounces
CONSTRUCTION:	Shell
SABOT:	Wooden cup (missing)
FUZING:	Bormann time fuze

DIAMETER:	4.52 inches
GUN:	12-pounder smooth-bore, 4.62-inch calibre
LENGTH:	—
WEIGHT:	11 pounds 1 ounce
CONSTRUCTION:	Case shot
SABOT:	Wooden cup (missing)
FUZING:	Confederate copy of the Bormann time fuze

DIAMETER:	4.49 inches
GUN:	12-pounder smooth-bore, 4.62-inch calibre
LENGTH:	—
WEIGHT:	8 pounds
CONSTRUCTION:	Shell
SABOT:	Wooden cup (missing)
FUZING:	Bormann time fuze

Note the star in the center of the Federal Bormann time fuze. This star is believed to signify manufacture at a particular arsenal. The authors know of several different arsenal marks found on other Bormann time fuzes. This example is non-excavated, and the Bormann time fuze is unpunched. The function of the Bormann time fuze is explained on page 21. A cross-section of a spherical case-shot projectile fitted with a Bormann time fuze can be found on page 10, figure II A-1.

Due to the repeated poor performance of the Confederate copy of the Bormann time fuze, its manufacture was discontinued by 1863. The remaining Bormann time fuzed projectiles were drilled and reamed in the center of the fuze to accept a paper time fuze that was inserted in the newly created fuze well. Often the face of the fuze was hammered flat, thus obliterating the numbers. These altered projectiles have been recovered from Honey Hill, South Carolina, and Augusta, Georgia. Examples have also been recovered in 6-pounder (3.67-inch calibre) smoothbore projectiles.

This Federal Bormann time fuze is unpunched and has raised dots instead of numbers, similar to the Braille system. As a result, this fuze is commonly referred to as a Bormann Braille time fuze. The dots are grouped, from one to five, in the location where the numbers would be on a standard-style Bormann fuze. No Confederate copies of this style of fuze have been recovered. Projectiles using this type of Bormann fuze are uncommon in any calibre.

Fig. III A-13
Confederate
Spherical

Fig. III A-14
Confederate
Spherical

Fig. III A-15
Federal
Spherical

DIAMETER:	4.47 inches
GUN:	12-pounder Coehorn mortar, 4.62-inch calibre
LENGTH:	—
WEIGHT:	7 pounds 10 ounces
CONSTRUCTION:	Shell
SABOT:	None
FUZING:	Wooden fuze plug, paper time fuze

Note the indentations, commonly referred to as tong holes, located on either side of the fuze hole. These tong holes were designed to aid in loading and aligning the projectile so that the fuze was in the center of the mortar's bore, opposite the powder charge. Federal Coehorn mortar projectiles were not manufactured with tong holes or ears.

DIAMETER:	5.63 inches
GUN:	24-pounder Coehorn mortar, 5.82-inch calibre
LENGTH:	—
WEIGHT:	16 pounds 4 ounces
CONSTRUCTION:	Shell
SABOT:	None
FUZING:	Wooden fuze plug, paper time fuze

The 24-pounder (5.82-inch calibre) Coehorn mortar is more common than the 12-pounder (4.62-inch calibre) size. In Abbot's book, *Siege Artillery In The Campaigns Against Richmond,* he stated the Federal forces should have employed the Confederate method of tong holes as opposed to the clumsy system of strapping with tin.

DIAMETER:	5.65 inches
GUN:	24-pounder Coehorn mortar, 5.82-inch calibre
LENGTH:	—
WEIGHT:	16 pounds 13 ounces
CONSTRUCTION:	Shell
SABOT:	None
FUZING:	Wooden fuze plug, paper time fuze

The Federals used two tin straps with loops on them to aid in loading and centering the projectile's fuze in the Coehorn mortar. The two straps cross underneath and wrap completely around the projectile, and the ends of the straps are passed through the slits of the collar, folded down, and set flat. Note that this specimen is missing a portion of one strap. This style of Coehorn mortar projectile was used extensively in the Petersburg, Virginia, Campaign.

Fig. III A-16
Confederate Spherical

Fig. III A-17
Confederate Spherical

Fig. III A-18
Confederate Spherical

DIAMETER:	4.52 inches
GUN:	12-pounder smoothbore, 4.62-inch calibre
LENGTH:	6/18 inches w/sabot
WEIGHT:	10 pounds 9 ounces
CONSTRUCTION:	Case shot
SABOT:	Wooden cup
FUZING:	Copper fuze plug, paper time fuze

DIAMETER:	4.50 inches
GUN:	12-pounder smoothbore, 4.62-inch calibre
WEIGHT:	9 pounds 10 ounces
CONSTRUCTION:	Case shot
SABOT:	Wooden sabot (missing)
FUZING:	Copper Bormann replacement fuze plug, paper time fuze

DIAMETER:	4.50 inches
GUN:	12-pounder smoothbore, 4.62-inch calibre
LENGTH:	—
WEIGHT:	9 pounds 14 ounces
CONSTRUCTION:	Case shot
SABOT:	Wooden cup (missing)
FUZING:	Copper fuze plug, paper time fuze

The lead side-loader ball above is non-excavated and rests on its original wooden sabot. The twine used to tighten the four tin straps is missing. Note that this wooden sabot is longer than the specimen on page 31, figure III A-8. This projectile, when equipped with this longer sabot variety, was designed to be fired from the 12-pounder howitzer cannon with its tapered chamber. The 12-pounder field howitzer, firing a spherical case-shot ball with a service charge of .75 pounds of powder at 3°, 45 minutes, had a range of 1,050 yards and a four-second time of flight.

Note that this smoothbore projectile has a Bormann replacement fuze plug and an iron side-loader plug. The Confederates discontinued the use of the Bormann fuze by 1863 and replaced it with an oversized copper fuze plug that screwed into the existing underplug threads. In an attempt to conserve lead, iron was used in the manufacture of the side-loading plug. The Bormann replacement fuze plug can also be found in 6-pounder (3.67-inch calibre) and 24-pounder (5.82-inch calibre).

Due to a shortage of lead the Confederates used iron, but there were problems. The standard method was to drill through the solidified case-shot balls and matrix to create the bursting cavity, but the iron balls made this difficult. The solution was to create the bursting cavity by inserting a dowel into the fuze opening. The iron balls were inserted through the hole on the projectile's side, and the hot, liquified matrix poured into the hole. After the matrix cooled, a lead, iron, copper, or brass plug was screwed into the loading hole. The powder was installed and the fuze plug screwed in. Projectiles with side-loader plugs made of copper or brass are uncommon.

Fig. III A-19
Federal
Conical

DIAMETER:	2.85 inches
GUN:	10-pounder Parrott rifle, 2.9-inch calibre
LENGTH:	7 inches
WEIGHT:	8 pounds
CONSTRUCTION:	Canister
SABOT:	Wooden cylinder
FUZING:	None

Standard canister is found with iron or lead balls stacked in tiers; the interstices are filled with dry, sifted sawdust, packed with a pointed stick so that the balls will hold by themselves. The wooden sabots found on field canisters have two grooves cut into them. The cartridge bag was tied onto these deep grooves in a complicated fashion. The canister cylinder was commonly made of tin, which was dipped into a lacquer of beeswax dissolved in spirits of turpentine to prevent rusting while in field service. This non-excavated example was the most common style of canister used by Federal artillery for the 10-pounder Parrott (2.9-inch calibre) rifled cannon.

Fig. III A-20
Federal
Conical

DIAMETER:	3.59 inches
GUN:	6-pounder smoothbore, 3.67-inch calibre
LENGTH:	6 7/8 inches
WEIGHT:	7 pounds 8 ounces
CONSTRUCTION:	Canister
SABOT:	Wooden cylinder
FUZING:	None

This specimen is non-excavated and is an example of the most common style of canister used in the 6-pounder (3.67-inch calibre) smoothbore cannon. It is 3" shorter than the standard-style 20-pounder canister, also for a 3.67-inch bore. Both Northern and Southern forces used this size canister. After attachment of the cartridge bag, which was tied to the deep grooves cut into the wooden sabot, the round was referred to as fixed ammunition. Note the vertical solder seam running the length of the tin cylinder.

Fig. III A-21
Federal
Conical

DIAMETER:	4.50 inches
GUN:	12-pounder smoothbore, 4.62-inch calibre
LENGTH:	8 inches
WEIGHT:	14 pounds 11 ounces
CONSTRUCTION:	Canister
SABOT:	Wooden cylinder
FUZING:	None

Canister was designed to be fired at close range with a resulting devastating effect on the enemy. This non-excavated specimen is the standard-style canister that both the Federal and Confederate forces used in the 12-pounder (4.62-inch calibre) smoothbore cannon. A 12-pounder field gun with a powder charge of 2.0 pounds, fired a 12-pounder canister with an initial muzzle velocity of 1,262 feet per second. See page 19, figure II A-19, for a reconstructed 12-pounder canister.

Fig. III A-22
Federal
Hotchkiss

Fig. III A-23
Federal
Hotchkiss

DIAMETER:	2.90 inches
GUN:	3-inch wrought iron (ordnance) rifle
LENGTH:	8 inches
WEIGHT:	7 pounds 1 ounce
CONSTRUCTION:	Canister
SABOT:	Lead cup
FUZING:	None

DIAMETER:	3.57 inches
GUN:	20-pounder Parrott rifle, 3.67-inch calibre
LENGTH:	10 inches
WEIGHT:	14 pounds
CONSTRUCTION:	Canister
SABOT:	Lead cup
FUZING:	None

This non-excavated canister has "HOTCHKISS 3 IN JAN'Y 7 1862 PATENT" molded in raised letters on the bottom of the lead base. Examples are found with tiers of iron or lead balls packed in dry, sifted sawdust. The canister cylinder is made of tinned sheet-iron, ordinarily known as tin-plate. Benjamin B. Hotchkiss patented this canister on January 7, 1862, patent #34,058.

Molded in raised letters on the bottom of the lead base are the letters "HOTCHKISS 3 67/100 JAN. 7TH 1862 PATENT". Upon firing, the Hotchkiss canister would often take the grooves of the cannon's rifling, creating an uneven dispersion of the canister balls. Addison M. Sawyer attempted to correct this problem with his rigid-cylindrical canister (see page 37, figure III A-24). This example was recovered near Petersburg, Virginia, at the site of the August 1864 City Point explosion.

Fig. III A-24
Federal
Sawyer

Fig. III A-25
Federal
Sawyer

DIAMETER:	3.62 inches
GUN:	Sawyer rifle, 3.67-inch calibre
LENGTH:	5 3/4 inches
WEIGHT:	3 pounds 3 ounces (filler balls missing)
CONSTRUCTION:	Canister
SABOT:	None
FUZING:	None

DIAMETER:	3.60 inches
GUN:	Sawyer rifle, 3.67-inch calibre
LENGTH:	5 13/16 inches
WEIGHT:	4 pounds 4 ounces (filler balls missing)
CONSTRUCTION:	Canister
SABOT:	None
FUZING:	None

This is correctly referred to as Sawyer's solid-shot canister. Addison M Sawyer patented this rigid cylindrical canister on November 19, 1861, patent #33,754. This canister was designed not to expand into the guns rifling, thus allowing for a more uniform dispersement of the canister balls. The Sawyer canister was designed so that it could be fired from a Sawyer rifle (3.67-inch calibre) or a 6-pounder smoothbore (3.67-inch calibre). The canister has three holes in the bottom, which allowed the propellant charge to help force out the canister balls. The majority of Sawyer canisters have been recovered from Port Hudson, Louisiana. This style of Sawyer canister is also found in 3.4-inch calibre.

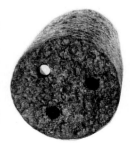

This is correctly referred to as Sawyer's accelerating canister. On November 16, 1861, 336 of these projectiles were delivered by Elmer Townsend & Company to the Federal Ordnance department. In the National Archives is a letter written to General A.B. Dyer, stating that this is a "six pounder accelerating canister" with a "wooden plug closing the mouth of the canister." The hole in the base (right) contained a powder train that ignited an explosive charge between the balls and the canister base. The charge was ignited after leaving the gun, extending the canister's range. The rigid-cylinder Sawyer canisters also acted as projectiles after the canister balls were dispersed.

37

Fig. III A-26
Federal
James Canister Pattern I

Fig. III A-27
Federal
James Canister Pattern I

DIAMETER:	3.70 inches
GUN:	14-pounder James rifle 3.8-inch calibre
LENGTH:	8 inches
WEIGHT:	13 pounds, 3 ounces
CONSTRUCTION:	Canister
SABOT:	Lead ring covered with a tin sleeve
FUZING:	None

DIAMETER:	3.63 inches
GUN:	14-pounder James rifle, 3.8-inch calibre
LENGTH:	3 1/2 inches
WEIGHT:	4 pounds 14 ounces
CONSTRUCTION:	Canister
SABOT:	Lead ring covered with a tin sleeve (missing)
FUZING:	None

This extremely rare excavated specimen illustrates the construction of the James canister. Note the iron canister balls exposed by the partially missing tin plate. A James Canister Pattern I sabot was used for the base. The placement of the tin sheeting over the lead sabot was an attempt to keep the lead from fouling the grooves of the rifled cannon during firing. The majority of James canisters have been recovered from Shiloh and Fort Pillow, Tennessee. This unfired pictured example was recovered from the April 1862 battlefield of Shiloh, Tennessee.

This is the base of a James canister similar to figure III A-26. It has been fired and, as usual, the lead covering has been stripped off. The cylindrical canister was attached with six copper nails through the holes noted on the top of the base. The holes in the bottom sides of the base helped attach the lead band to the ribs. The canister base also acted as a projectile after leaving the cannon. James canisters are rare. This specimen was recovered from Fort Pillow, Tennessee.

Fig. III A-28
Federal
James Hot Shot Pattern I

Fig. III A-29
Federal
James Hot Shot Pattern I

DIAMETER:	3.63 inches
GUN:	6-pounder rifle and/or smoothbore, 3.67-inch calibre
LENGTH:	3 3/4 inches (base only)
WEIGHT:	4 pounds 5 ounces (base only)
CONSTRUCTION:	Hot shot base
SABOT:	Lead ring covered with a tin sleeve (missing)
FUZING:	None

DIAMETER:	4.45 inches
GUN:	12-pounder rifle and/or smoothbore, 4.62-inch calibre
LENGTH:	4 1/6 inches
WEIGHT:	7 pounds 14 ounces
CONSTRUCTION:	Hot shot base
SABOT:	Lead ring covered with a tin sleeve (missing)
FUZING:	None

This iron hot shot base was patented by Charles T. James, patent #34,950, on April 15, 1862. The iron base was designed to keep the red-hot projectile from making contact with the powder charge in the cannon, which could cause a premature discharge. It was used in a 3.67-inch rifled cannon and could also be fired from a 6-pounder (3.67-inch calibre) smoothbore cannon. An added feature with this design is that upon firing the iron base itself became a projectile, thereby inflicting greater damage. Note the spherical 6-pounder (3.67-inch calibre) solid shot in the photograph that illustrates how the red-hot ball rested on the base.

This rare James sub-pattern hot shot base was recovered from the Battle of Shiloh, Tennessee, which took place in April 1862. A red-hot 12-pounder solid shot projectile was intended to be used with this iron base. This specimen appears to be the only example known. James also obtained patent #34,965, on April 15, 1862, for a similarly constructed base for a 6-pounder (3.67-inch calibre) Bormann-fuzed spherical projectile. To the authors' knowledge the base described in this patent was not manufactured.

Fig. III A-30
Confederate
Stand of grape

Fig. III A-31
Pre-war Federal
Quilted grape

DIAMETER:	4.60 inches
GUN:	12-pounder smoothbore, 4.62-inch calibre
LENGTH:	5 13/16 inches to top plate
WEIGHT:	14 pounds 6 ounces
CONSTRUCTION:	Grape shot
SABOT:	None
FUZING:	None

DIAMETER:	2.74 inches
GUN:	3-pounder smoothbore, 2.9-inch calibre
LENGTH:	8 inches
WEIGHT:	8 pounds 12 ounces
CONSTRUCTION:	Quilted grape
SABOT:	Wooden cylinder
FUZING:	None

This non-excavated specimen is referred to as a stand of grape. The Federal forces discontinued the 12-pounder stand of grape prior to 1861 and replaced it with canister. The shot used in canisters was large enough to be effective and possessed the advantage of striking a great many more points on impact than grape. Stands of grape are also found in the following field calibres: 18-pounder (5.3-inch calibre), and 24-pounder (5.82-inch calibre). Note the crude mold seams on the iron balls which point to Confederate manufacture. Three complete 12-pounder stands were recovered from Vicksburg, Mississippi. Complete excavated specimens are extremely rare.

This pre-war grapeshot projectile consisted of a wooden base with a rod centered like a bolt around which lead balls were piled in tiers. It was then completely enclosed in canvas and a heavy twine (sometimes wire) stitched between the balls, giving the projectile its distinctive quilted-like appearance. *Cooper's Tactics* (1845) stated that the Federal forces continued the use of the 3-pounder smoothbore cannon into the 1820s as a light field artillery piece. According to De Tousard's *American Artillerist's Companion* (1809) and Duane's *Military Dictionary* (1810), tests showed that the 3- and 4-pounder quilted grapeshot was accurate and dependable at 400-500 yards. At less than 400 yards, case-shot and canister were more effective, primarily because of better dispersement. The early quilted grape contained lead balls but they deformed too much upon ignition of the powder charge. Lead balls were later replaced with iron. This example has thirty-five one-inch lead balls and is located in the West Point Military Academy Museum.

Fig. III A-32
Confederate
Archer

Fig. III A-33
Confederate
Archer

DIAMETER:	2.94 inches
GUN:	3-inch rifle
LENGTH:	5 11/16 inches
WEIGHT:	7 pounds 4 ounces
CONSTRUCTION:	Solid shot
SABOT:	Lead band
FUZING:	None

DIAMETER:	2.94 inches
GUN:	3-inch rifle
LENGTH:	5 11/16 inches
WEIGHT:	5 pounds 15 ounces
CONSTRUCTION:	Solid shot
SABOT:	Lead band (missing)
FUZING:	None

Archer projectiles were named after Dr. Junius L. Archer, owner of the Bellona Foundry, which was located in Virginia. This projectile has two deep grooves on the tapered cone portion of the body to help hold the lead sabot in during firing. The majority of the fired Archer projectiles are found with the lead sabot missing. In the space between the lead band and the projectile body was a lubricated hemp rope. During firing, this hemp rope was forced into the grooves of the cannon when the lead sabot expanded. The lubricant reduced friction and subsequent wear on the cannon. Similar specimens have been found in 3.3-inch calibre.

Note the two grooves on the tapered cone portion of the projectile body, which held the lead sabot in place during expansion. This is the same pattern as the Archer in figure III A-32, but without the lead sabot. A large number of Archer projectiles were manufactured at the Bellona Foundry; they were also manufactured in other deep South locations, including Selma Arsenal in Alabama. Examples of this variety of the Archer pattern have been recovered from the April 1862 battlefield of Shiloh, Tennessee.

Fig. III A-34
Confederate Archer

Fig. III A-35
Confederate Archer

DIAMETER:	2.93 inches
GUN:	3-inch rifle
LENGTH:	6 inches
WEIGHT:	7 pounds 13 ounces
CONSTRUCTION:	Solid shot
SABOT:	Lead band
FUZING:	None

DIAMETER:	2.94 inches
GUN:	3-inch rifle
LENGTH:	6 inches
WEIGHT:	7 pounds 5 ounces
CONSTRUCTION:	Solid shot
SABOT:	Lead band (missing)
FUZING:	None

Note the lubrication groove between the lead band and the body of the projectile. A lubricant was applied to the linen or canvas that covered the lead band. This helped to prevent the bore of the cannon from being fouled with the lead from the sabot. Several Archer projectiles similar to the variety shown have been recovered from the June 1864 Battle of Kennesaw Mountain, Georgia.

Note the two deep grooves on the tapered cone portion of the projectile body and the distinct casting flaw on the projectile's iron body. This fired Archer is similar to that in figure III A-34, but without the lead sabot. This Archer variety is believed by the authors to be one of the most common Archer projectiles known. Projectiles of this variety have been recovered from the April 1862 Shiloh, Tennessee, battlefield.

Fig. III A-36
Confederate Archer

Fig. III A-37
Confederate Archer

DIAMETER:	2.94 inches
GUN:	3-inch rifle
LENGTH:	6 inches
WEIGHT:	8 pounds 7 ounces
CONSTRUCTION:	Solid shot
SABOT:	Lead band
FUZING:	None

DIAMETER:	2.94 inches
GUN:	3-inch rifle
LENGTH:	6 inches
WEIGHT:	7 pounds 8 ounces
CONSTRUCTION:	Solid shot
SABOT:	Lead band (missing)
FUZING:	None

This unfired Archer variant has a small flat nose. It is less common than the pointed-nose variety. The tapered cone portion of the projectile body has two grooves that helped hold the lead band on during firing. This particular variety of the Archer series has been recovered from several Virginia battlefields, including Fairfax, Virginia.

This fired projectile is similar to that in figure III A-36, with a small flat nose and two grooves on the tapered cone. This specimen was recovered from the April 1862 battlefield of Shiloh, Tennessee. The Confederates had only seven 3-inch rifles engaged during the Battle of Shiloh. These 3-inch rifles were found in the following units of the Army of Mississippi: Stanford's Mississippi Battery, Gage's Alabama Battery, Hubbard's Arkansas Battery, and Pettus's Mississippi Flying Artillery.

Fig. III A-38
Confederate
Archer

Fig. III A-39
Confederate
Archer

DIAMETER:	2.94 inches
GUN:	3-inch rifle
LENGTH:	5 3/4 inches
WEIGHT:	6 pounds 4 ounces
CONSTRUCTION:	Shell
SABOT:	Lead band
FUZING:	Wooden fuze plug, paper time fuze

DIAMETER:	2.94 inches
GUN:	3-inch rifle
LENGTH:	5 7/8 inches
WEIGHT:	5 pounds 3 ounces
CONSTRUCTION:	Shell
SABOT:	Lead band (missing)
FUZING:	Wooden fuze plug, paper time fuze

This unfired Archer has two vertical flame grooves on the iron projectile body. The lead sabot is also narrower than those found on most Archer projectiles. Note the wooden fuze plug in the nose of the projectile. Archer projectiles were named after Dr. Junius L. Archer, owner of the Bellona Foundry, which was located in Virginia. This particular Archer was manufactured at the Selma Arsenal in Alabama and was recovered at that site.

The lead sabot is missing on this example, which is typical of recovered fired Archer projectiles. This projectile is similar to that in figure III A-38. Note that the well-preserved wooden fuze plug is still intact. There are two vertical flame grooves on the projectile body, designed to help the propellant flame reach the paper time fuze. In *The Long Arm of Lee*, Jennings Wise mentions that Archer projectiles, when fired, did not fly point foremost but tumbled and had no effective range.

Fig. III A-40
Confederate Archer

DIAMETER:	2.97 inches
GUN:	3-inch rifle
LENGTH:	7 3/16 inches
WEIGHT:	8 pounds 11 ounces
CONSTRUCTION:	Shell
SABOT:	Lead band
FUZING:	Wooden fuze plug, paper time fuze

This unfired Archer projectile has one groove and four vertical flanges to help hold the lead sabot on the projectile during firing. A small additional bottom ring or groove can be seen at the base of the projectile body. Note the hemp rope, which was greased to help decrease the amount of friction generated in the bore of the cannon. This variety of Archer projectile has been recovered from Virginia battlefields.

Fig. III A-41
Confederate Archer

DIAMETER:	2.94 inches
GUN:	3-inch rifle
LENGTH:	7 1/4 inches
WEIGHT:	7 pounds 4 ounces
CONSTRUCTION:	Shell
SABOT:	Lead band (missing)
FUZING:	Wooden fuze plug, paper time fuze

This fired example of an Archer projectile is of the same variety as that shown in figure III A-40, but without the lead sabot. This shell was most likely manufactured at the Bellona Foundry, which was located fourteen miles above Richmond, Virginia, and was adjacent to the Bellona Arsenal. The Bellona Arsenal served as a facility for assembly and repair of small-arms and other ordnance. The Arsenal also received and stored cannon produced by the Bellona Foundry.

Fig. III A-42
Confederate
Archer

Fig. III A-43
Confederate
Archer

DIAMETER:	3.26 inches
GUN:	3.3-inch Confederate rifle
LENGTH:	6 1/2 inches
WEIGHT:	12 pounds 1 ounce
CONSTRUCTION:	Solid shot
SABOT:	Lead band
FUZING:	None

DIAMETER:	3.22 inches
GUN:	3.3-inch Confederate rifle
LENGTH:	6 1/2 inches
WEIGHT:	8 pounds 14 ounces
CONSTRUCTION:	Solid shot
SABOT:	Lead band (missing)
FUZING:	None

Note that the lower portion of this iron projectile body is cylindrical and not tapered, which is uncommon in the Archer pattern of projectiles. The lead sabot extends to the base of the projectile, which is also unusual. This projectile was recovered from the April 1862 Battle of Shiloh, Tennessee. Similar specimens were fired by the 5th Company, Washington Artillery of New Orleans, Louisiana. Leeds and Company of New Orleans, Louisiana, delivered to the Confederacy a total of seventeen 3.3-inch bronze rifles between October 1861 and April 1862. Three surviving cannon showing a seven-groove rifling pattern can be found at the United States Military Academy Museum at West Point, New York.

This fired Archer projectile is similar to that shown in figure III A-42 but is missing the lead sabot, which was typically lost during firing. Note that on the straight cylindrical base there are three grooves to help hold the lead sabot on the tapered base. This Archer projectile variety was recovered from the 1862 battlefield of Shiloh, Tennessee.

Fig. III A-44
Confederate
Archer

Fig. III A-45
Confederate
Archer

DIAMETER:	3.26 inches
GUN:	3.3-inch Confederate rifle
LENGTH:	5 1/4 inches
WEIGHT:	7 pounds 14 ounces
CONSTRUCTION:	Shell
SABOT:	Lead band
FUZING:	Wooden fuze plug, paper time fuze

DIAMETER:	3.23 inches
GUN:	3.3-inch Confederate rifle
LENGTH:	5 1/4 inches
WEIGHT:	5 pounds 10 ounces
CONSTRUCTION:	Shell
SABOT:	Lead band (missing)
FUZING:	Wooden fuze plug, paper time fuze

This unfired Archer projectile variety was manufactured without flame grooves. Similar specimens, however, have been recovered with flame grooves (see figure III A-45). There are three grooves and two small vertical flanges on the tapered base. The purpose of this arrangement was to increase the chances of the sabot remaining on the projectile body during firing. Note the prominent expansion and lubrication groove, which is missing the lubricated hemp rope used to reduce friction during firing.

This fired Archer projectile is similar to the variety shown in figure III A-44 but is missing the lead sabot. It has two small vertical flame grooves opposite each other on the untapered portion of the projectile body. Note the crude casting flaw in the center of the projectile body, typical of Confederate-manufactured projectiles.

Fig. III A-46
Great Britain
Armstrong

Fig. III A-47
Great Britain
Armstrong

Fig. III A-48
Great Britain
Armstrong

DIAMETER:	3.05 inches
GUN:	12-pounder Armstrong breechloading rifle, 3-inch calibre
LENGTH:	8 9/16 inches
WEIGHT:	11 pounds 1 ounce
CONSTRUCTION:	Shell
SABOT:	Lead jacket
FUZING:	CS copper fuze plug, paper time fuze

This projectile consists of a thin cast iron shell enclosing forty-two segment-shaped pieces of cast iron, built up so as to form a cylindrical center cavity. The exterior of the shell is thinly coated with lead, which was allowed to percolate among the segments to fill up the interstices; the central cavity was kept open by a steel rod. The projectile was so compact that it could be fired through six feet of hard timber, yet its resistance to a bursting charge was so small that less than one ounce of powder was required to burst it. The Confederates had the exclusive use of this Armstrong-pattern projectile. Ten unfired Armstrongs were recovered in a Confederate fort at High Bridge, Virginia.

DIAMETER:	2.95 inches
GUN:	12-pounder Armstrong muzzle-loading rifle, 3-inch calibre
LENGTH:	9 1/8 inches
WEIGHT:	10 pounds 8 ounces
CONSTRUCTION:	Segmented interior
SABOT:	Triple rows of three brass studs
FUZING:	None; shipping plug

This unfired example of the longer variety of the 3-inch calibre shunted Armstrong projectile has triple rows of three brass studs. Located in the threaded fuze well is a brass shipping plug, which was removed prior to charging and fuzing the projectile.

DIAMETER:	2.96 inches
GUN:	12-pounder Armstrong muzzle-loading rifle, 3-inch calibre
LENGTH:	7 1/5 inches
WEIGHT:	10 pounds 12 ounces
CONSTRUCTION:	Segmented interior
SABOT:	Double rows of three brass studs
FUZING:	None; shipping plug

This unfired example of the British Armstrong projectile is located in the United States Military Academy Museum at West Point, New York. The shorter variety of the 3-inch Armstrong shunt shells has double rows of three brass studs. The interior is in the form of iron segments arranged around a central channel which held the bursting charge.

The Confederates fired one projectile of the pattern shown in Fig. III A-46 into General Abbot's Dutch Gap batteries in 1864. Abbot stated: "Had it not been for this circumstance, I should have supposed that none of the ordnance of this gun-maker was ever used by either army in Virginia."

Fig. III A-49
Great Britain
Blakely

Fig. III A-50
Great Britain
Blakely

DIAMETER:	3.42 inches across flats
GUN:	12-pounder Blakely rifle, 3.5-inch calibre
LENGTH:	7 11/16 inches
WEIGHT:	11 pounds 11 ounces
CONSTRUCTION:	Shell
SABOT:	None
FUZING:	Britten percussion, brass

DIAMETER:	3.93 inches across flats, 4.22 inches across flanges
GUN:	18-pounder Blakely rifle, 4-inch calibre
LENGTH:	9 1/8 inches
WEIGHT:	17 pounds 11 ounces
CONSTRUCTION:	Shell
SABOT:	None
FUZING:	Britten percussion, brass

This pattern has been mistakenly called the Preston projectile, after the name of its manufacturer: Fawcett, Preston & Company of Liverpool, England, which under Blakely's patent produced 12-pounder (3.5-inch calibre) Blakely rifles in 1860-1861. This projectile pattern was patented by Theophilus Alexander Blakely, British patent #1,286, dated May 22, 1863. This example has a flat base and six vertical inclined flanges to allow it to fit the Blakely rifle's sawtooth rifling. The poor design of the Britten fuze caused many shells to be rendered harmless upon firing. The majority of the battlefield-recovered 12-pounder (3.5-inch calibre) Blakely projectiles have come from the 1863 Siege of Port Hudson, Louisiana.

Some 18-pounder, (4-inch calibre) Blakely projectiles were fired by the Confederate artillery during the defenses of Charleston, South Carolina. It was used only by the Confederate forces, and even then in extremely limited quantities. On Tuesday, September 15, 1863, Edward Manigault's journal entry stated: "Fired also 4 Shell with the 4 in. Blakely Gun. The results were unsatisfactory. The projectiles flew very wildly. Elevations 13, 14, 15, & 16 1/2 [degrees]."

Fig. III A-51
Great Britain
Britten

Fig. III A-52
Great Britain
Britten

DIAMETER:	3.45 inches
GUN:	12-pounder Blakely rifle, 3.5-inch calibre
LENGTH:	5 7/8 inches
WEIGHT:	11 pounds 8 ounces
CONSTRUCTION:	Solid shot
SABOT:	Lead cup
FUZING:	None

DIAMETER:	3.44 inches
GUN:	12-pounder Blakely rifle, 3.5-inch calibre
LENGTH:	7 1/4 inches
WEIGHT:	12 pounds 2 ounces
CONSTRUCTION:	Shell, segmented interior
SABOT:	Lead cup
FUZING:	Britten percussion

This is an example of the standard-style shot for the 12-pounder (3.5-inch calibre) Blakely rifled cannon. According to Bashley Britten's British patent #1740, dated August 1, 1855, "The method of coating the projectiles with soft metal in such a manner as to stand the explosive force of the powder is as follows:—The iron is first coated with zinc by the process commonly known as the galvanising process, and while sufficiently hot to keep the zinc in a fuzed state on its surface, it is plunged into a mould or vessel of suitable form containing the lead or other soft metal in a fuzed state, and then allowed to get cold." Fired specimens have nearly always been found with their lead sabots intact.

Bashley Britten patented this projectile's segmented interior construction, British patent #585, dated March 8, 1861. It reads, in part: "I construct this projectile in the following manner:—I make a core of loam or sand of such form as to fill the interior space. Round this core I place numerous pieces shaped and arranged somewhat like the natural divisions of an orange. Each of theses pieces is cast with several cores or plates partially dividing them so as to weaken them at those places, that they may easily break up when the shell explodes. The surfaces of these pieces are dressed over with a coating of loam or such like material, and they are bound round with a wire, or otherwise secured round the inner core of sand....Round this combined core I cast the external shell, which may be of iron or other suitable metal." The interior has nine long wedges of iron with lines of weakness cast in each wedge. Ideally, the bursting charge broke the wedges into fifty-four fragments, and the outer shell fragmented as well.

Fig. III A-53
Confederate Brooke

DIAMETER:	2.94 inches
GUN:	3-inch Parrott rifle
LENGTH:	7 7/8 inches
WEIGHT:	8 pounds 12 ounces
CONSTRUCTION:	Shell
SABOT:	Copper rachet plate
FUZING:	Wooden fuze plug, paper time fuze

This projectile was named after its inventor, Commander John M. Brooke, C.S.N., and is commonly called a rebated Brooke. There are six ratchets in the copper sabot that correspond to the six cast-in ratchets on the shell base. A single square-headed bolt holds the sabot on. The purpose of the rebated section (reduced diameter) was to decrease the amount of surface area that needed to be turned on a lathe. Specimens have been recovered in Nashville, Tennessee, and in the Atlanta, Georgia, area.

Fig. III A-54
Confederate Brooke

DIAMETER:	2.85 inches
GUN:	10-pounder Parrott rifle, 2.9-inch calibre
LENGTH:	9 inches
WEIGHT:	10 pounds 1 ounce
CONSTRUCTION:	Shell
SABOT:	Copper rachet plate
FUZING:	Wooden fuze plug, paper time fuze

This is an example of the most common 10-pounder (2.9-inch calibre) Brooke projectile recovered. It was turned on a lathe from the sabot to the ogive. Lathing was needed to turn the projectile casting down to the dimensions needed to properly fit into the bore of the cannon. The thin-walled copper sabot tended to break as it expanded into the grooves of the cannon. In an attempt to correct this problem, the sabot was made thicker and pre-cast with the rifling grooves, as can be seen in figure III A-55. The example above was recovered from the June 1864 Battlefield of Kennesaw Mountain, Georgia.

Fig. III A-55
Confederate Brooke

DIAMETER:	2.84 inches
GUN:	10-pounder Parrott rifle, 2.9-inch calibre
LENGTH:	9 3/16 inches
WEIGHT:	9 pounds 10 ounces
CONSTRUCTION:	Shell
SABOT:	Copper rachet plate
FUZING:	Copper fuze plug, paper time fuze

The sabot on this projectile is pre-cast with three flanges to fit the gun's grooves. This was done in an attempt to correct the problem with the thinner copper sabots breaking during detonation of the cannon. When fired, the ratchets tightened against each other, equally absorbing the energy and thus increasing the sabot's stability. The copper time fuze plug is slotted. This projectile variety was used exclusively by Forrest's Artillery (Morton's Battery) and then only in north Alabama and Mississippi battlefields. This specimen was recovered from Sulphur Trestle, Alabama. This variety of the Brooke pattern is extremely rare.

Fig. III A-56
Confederate
Broun

Fig. III A-57
Confederate
Broun

Fig. III A-58
Confederate
Broun

DIAMETER:	2.94 inches
GUN:	3-inch rifle
LENGTH:	7 1/2 inches
WEIGHT:	9 pounds 4 ounces
CONSTRUCTION:	Shell (possible lines of weakness)
SABOT:	Copper ring
FUZING:	Wooden fuze plug, paper time fuze

DIAMETER:	2.94 inches
GUN:	3-inch rifle
LENGTH:	8 1/4 inches
WEIGHT:	9 pounds 1 ounces
CONSTRUCTION:	Shell, lines of weakness
SABOT:	Copper ring
FUZING:	Wooden fuze plug, paper time fuze

DIAMETER:	3.61 inches
GUN:	3.67-inch calibre rifle
LENGTH:	5 1/2 inches
WEIGHT:	8 pounds 12 ounces
CONSTRUCTION:	Shell, lines of weakness
SABOT:	Copper ring
FUZING:	Wooden fuze plug, paper time fuze

Lieutenant Colonel W. L. Broun, commander of the Richmond Arsenal beginning in June 1863, is considered to be the developer of this projectile pattern. Since the copper sabot was designed to serve as a bourrelet, only one bearing surface was needed on the projectile body. The bourrelet and the sabot were machined on a lathe to the proper tolerance. This example is of the short variety; the longer version is approximately 3/4" longer. There are two saw cuts to aid in the expansion of the sabot into the gun's grooves. Most fired specimens have the high, thin sabot blown off, revealing the slightly rounded base of the body. Brouns are found mainly on late-war battlefields.

The interior of this Broun sub-pattern projectile is cast with lines of weakness in the configuration of a six-sided prism. Upon detonation, the shell was designed to break into twenty-four fragments of equal size, plus the nose and base. This projectile was recovered near the site of its manufacture, the Selma Arsenal in Alabama. Note that the projectile has only one raised bearing ring, which is located in the middle of the projectile. This location of the bearing surface is unusual for Broun-manufactured projectiles; typically the bourrelet is located closer to the nose. Other examples of this sub-pattern have been recovered from Johnsonville and Shiloh, Tennessee.

It is generally believed that this Broun projectile variety would have tumbled in flight due to its inadequate length-to-calibre ratio. The acceptable length of a rifled projectile is two and a half to three times the calibre of the gun. This projectile has twelve rectangular sections with lines of weakness cast in. The interior was designed to fragment upon detonation into equal-size pieces, with the exception of the nose and base. Note the lathe marks on the single bourrelet and high copper sabot. This example is unfired and was recovered from an Alabama site.

Fig. III A-59
Federal
Dyer

DIAMETER: 2.91 inches
GUN: 3-inch wrought iron (ordnance) rifle
LENGTH: 7 3/8 inches
WEIGHT: 8 pounds 5 ounces
CONSTRUCTION: Shell
SABOT: Lead cup
FUZING: Schenkl percussion, brass

This projectile was correctly named after its inventor, General Alexander B. Dyer. Federal government records indicate that William Sellers and Company manufactured 107,230 3-inch Dyer projectiles under their Federal ordnance contracts from September 26, 1861, through May 24, 1862. The pattern is found in case-shot and common shell. This Dyer pattern sabot is found with and without flame grooves. The majority of the specimens were fired from Federal artillery positions, although some were captured and subsequently used by the Confederate artillery. The brass percussion fuze has Schenkl's patent date stamped on the face.

Fig. III A-60
Federal
Dyer

DIAMETER: 2.93 inches
GUN: 3-inch wrought iron (ordnance) rifle
LENGTH: 7 1/8 inches
WEIGHT: 10 pounds 9 ounces
CONSTRUCTION: Case shot
SABOT: Lead cup
FUZING: Zinc fuze plug, paper time fuze

This Gettysburg-recovered Dyer has four flame grooves cast into the lead sabot. Note the lubrication groove above the sabot. Often the lead sabot of the 3-inch Dyer projectile became separated during firing. According to an October 28, 1864, letter in the National Archives from Major J.G. Benton to General Alexander B. Dyer, this problem was corrected: "...the old cups can be easily removed and good ones put on at a cost to the Government of 15 cents. There are about 55,000 of these projectiles at this Arsenal and I think that they can be made serviceable by Mr. Taylor's plan....Forty projectiles arranged in this way were fired without a single failure or detachment of the sabot."

Fig. III A-61
Federal
Dyer

DIAMETER: 2.94 inches
GUN: 3-inch wrought iron (ordnance) rifle
LENGTH: 7 1/2 inches
WEIGHT: 10 pounds
CONSTRUCTION: Case shot
SABOT: Lead cup
FUZING: Zinc fuze plug, paper time fuze

Some Dyer projectiles of this variety have been recovered with the brass Schenkl percussion fuze. This Dyer projectile's nose is more tapered than that in figure III A-60. This rare variation is found in both common shell and case shot. There are four flame grooves cast into the sabot. Note the lubrication and expansion groove above the sabot. Specimens have been recovered from Vicksburg, Mississippi, and Jenkins Ferry, Missouri.

Fig. III A-62
Federal
Hotchkiss

Fig. III A-63
Federal
Hotchkiss

DIAMETER:	2.94 inches
GUN:	3-inch wrought iron (ordnance) rifle
LENGTH:	7 1/4 inches
WEIGHT:	10 pounds 1 ounce
CONSTRUCTION:	Solid shot
SABOT:	Lead band
FUZING:	None

DIAMETER:	2.94 inches
GUN:	3-inch wrought iron (ordnance) rifle
LENGTH:	—
WEIGHT:	—
CONSTRUCTION:	Solid shot
SABOT:	Lead band
FUZING:	None

Andrew Hotchkiss patented this pattern of projectile on October 16, 1855, patent #13,679. His patent states that "shot consisting of three parts, two of which parts are of hard metal and the other of some flexible expansible material in the form of a band or ring attached to one of the hard-metal parts and overlapping the edge of the other, in such manner that either by the act of loading or of firing, or of both, the said ring shall take the impression of the grooves and be made to fit the bore, as described." In all Hotchkiss patterns used during the Civil War, the flexible expansible material was lead. Andrew Hotchkiss died in 1858.

This disassembled view shows the three-piece construction of the Hotchkiss projectile (the nose, the lead band, and the base cup). Upon the ignition of the gun, the base cup was driven along the cylindrical base of the projectile body, expanding the lead band (sabot) into the rifling. Hotchkiss patent projectiles were intended for use in the 3-inch wrought iron (ordnance) rifle, because the seven lands and grooves allowed a more even distribution of the stress during the expansion of the lead sabot.

Fig. III A-64
Federal
Hotchkiss

Fig. III A-65
Federal
Hotchkiss

Fig. III A-66
Federal
Hotchkiss

DIAMETER:	2.94 inches
GUN:	3-inch wrought iron (ordnance) rifle
LENGTH:	7 1/8 inches
WEIGHT:	9 pounds
CONSTRUCTION:	Case shot
SABOT:	Lead band
FUZING:	Lead fuze plug, paper time fuze

This unfired Hotchkiss projectile is of early manufacture, as evidenced by the absence of flame grooves. When the projectile was fired, the expanding lead band (sabot) sometimes sealed the bore so well that no flame could pass, thereby keeping the shell's paper time fuze from igniting. This led to the development of flame grooves, patented by Benjamin Berkeley Hotchkiss on June 7, 1864, patent #43,027. Some early war Hotchkiss shells do not have flame grooves and are found with metal fuze plugs. There are two round spanner holes on the top of the lead fuze plug to aid in its installation, rather than the usual slotted variety.

DIAMETER:	2.94 inches
GUN:	3-inch wrought iron (ordnance) rifle
LENGTH:	6 7/8 inches
WEIGHT:	8 pounds 3 ounces
CONSTRUCTION:	Shell
SABOT:	Lead band
FUZING:	Hotchkiss brass fuze plug, paper time fuze

More 3-inch Hotchkiss shells of this particular pattern were manufactured than any other style of Hotchkiss projectile during the Civil War. Specimens have been found with Hotchkiss's patent date application on the base cup: "HOTCHKISS PAT. OCT. 9, 1855." Note the original black arsenal paint on this unfired, non-excavated specimen. See page 13, figure II A-8, for an example of a Hotchkiss case-shot projectile's interior.

DIAMETER:	2.94 inches
GUN:	3-inch wrought iron (ordnance) rifle
LENGTH:	6 5/8 inches
WEIGHT:	8 pounds 7 ounces
CONSTRUCTION:	Shell
SABOT:	Lead band
FUZING:	Hotchkiss percussion, brass

No flame grooves were needed for percussion-fuzed shells since they were designed to explode on impact. Hotchkiss projectiles in this calibre were manufactured for use in the 3-inch wrought iron (ordnance) rifle and not the 3-inch Parrott rifle. Benjamin Berkeley Hotchkiss patented the brass percussion fuze on February 24, 1863, patent #37,756. See page 13, figure II A-7, for a cross-section of this Hotchkiss variety.

Fig. III A-67
Federal
Hotchkiss

Fig. III A-68
Federal
Hotchkiss

DIAMETER:	2.94 inches
GUN:	3-inch wrought iron (ordnance) rifle
LENGTH:	6 5/16 inches
WEIGHT:	9 pounds 8 ounces
CONSTRUCTION:	Shell
SABOT:	Lead band
FUZING:	Hotchkiss brass fuze plug, paper time fuze

DIAMETER:	2.94 inches
GUN:	3-inch wrought iron (ordnance) rifle
LENGTH:	6 1/4 inches
WEIGHT:	9 pounds 1 ounce
CONSTRUCTION:	Case shot
SABOT:	Lead band
FUZING:	Combination of Hotchkiss percussion and 14-second Hotchkiss-Bormann time fuze

This unfired Hotchkiss projectile is of a late-war production. The flat nose is fitted with a standard brass Hotchkiss time fuze plug. The body of the shell has three flame grooves which aided the propellant flame in reaching the paper time fuze. The slightly rounded base cup does not have the Hotchkiss patent date cast into it, as is commonly seen in other earlier production Hotchkiss projectiles. Specimens have been recovered in Nashville, Tennessee, and at Spanish Fort, Alabama.

Benjamin Berkeley Hotchkiss patented an improvement for the Hotchkiss projectile on May 16, 1865, patent #47,725. According to his patent, a wooden disk was to be inserted between the base cup and the base of the nose to decrease the risk of premature fracture of the shell during initial firing. The insufficient burning time of the standard-style Federal 5 1/4-second Bormann time fuze led to the development of the 14-second version for rifled ordnance. The protective cover of the Hotchkiss combination fuze pictured here was not removed prior to firing. The Hotchkiss sub-pattern projectile with a rounded base has been recovered from late-war battlefields such as Petersburg, Virginia. See page 87, figure III B-6, for more information on this fuzing system.

Fig. III A-69
Federal
Hotchkiss

Fig. III A-70
Federal
Hotchkiss

Fig. III A-71
Federal
Hotchkiss

DIAMETER:	3.74 inches
GUN:	14-pounder James rifle, 3.8-inch calibre
LENGTH:	6 7/8 inches
WEIGHT:	14 pounds 4 ounces
CONSTRUCTION:	Case shot
SABOT:	Lead band
FUZING:	Hotchkiss brass fuze plug, paper time fuze

DIAMETER:	3.73 inches
GUN:	14-pounder James rifle, 3.8-inch calibre
LENGTH:	7 inches
WEIGHT:	13 pounds 7 ounces
CONSTRUCTION:	Shell
SABOT:	Lead band
FUZING:	Percussion, iron anvil cap

DIAMETER:	3.73 inches
GUN:	14-pounder James rifle, 3.8-inch calibre
LENGTH:	7 1/8 inches
WEIGHT:	13 pounds 2 ounces (balls missing)
CONSTRUCTION:	Case shot
SABOT:	Lead band
FUZING:	Zinc fuze plug, paper time fuze

Specimens in this calibre have been noted with and without flame grooves. This projectile is an example of a Hotchkiss pattern that was manufactured to replace the poorly designed James projectile pattern. This Hotchkiss pattern is found in both case-shot and common shell varieties. The case-shot variety has a more rounded nose than the shell. The projectile shown was recovered from the 1863 Siege of Vicksburg, Mississippi. It also has been recovered in a 3.67-inch calibre size.

Percussion Hotchkiss projectiles were manufactured without flame grooves since they were designed to detonate on impact. This Hotchkiss projectile has an iron anvil cap percussion fuze that was patented by C.W. Smith and T.D. Stetson on March 25, 1862, patent #34,788. This fuze design was first used at West Point, New York, on its test range for artillery projectiles and cannon, and it is commonly referred to as a West Point-type percussion fuze.

C.W. Smith, G.H. Babcock, and B.B. and C.A. Hotchkiss were issued patent #38,359 on April 28, 1863, for an improvement in the Hotchkiss case-shot projectile: an iron plate that separated the bursting charge from the case-shot chamber. The plate was meant to decrease the chances of a premature discharge during firing. For easy insertion of the plate, the removable nose was developed. As a bonus, this allowed easier loading of the bursting charge and case-shot balls. The removable nose piece has two spanner holes opposite each other near the fuze well. The removable nose is machined with fine threads that screwed into threads on the projectile body.

Fig. III A-72
Confederate (copy)
James Pattern I, Sub-pattern I

DIAMETER:	3.21 inches
GUN:	3.3-inch Confederate rifle
LENGTH:	7 3/4 inches
WEIGHT:	11 pounds 9 ounces
CONSTRUCTION:	Solid shot
SABOT:	Lead ring
FUZING:	None

Note that this pictured example is unfired with the lead ring intact. This pattern projectile was an attempt by the Confederates to copy the James Pattern I, Sub-pattern I, solid shot. The projectile has a hollow base that allowed the explosive charge of the cannon to expand the lead ring into the grooves of the rifle. This Confederate James copy pattern is extremely rare and is the only attempt made by the Confederates to copy the Federal James projectile pattern. The majority of the recovered specimens have come from the 1862 Battle of Shiloh, Tennessee. Leeds and Company of New Orleans, Louisiana, delivered to the Confederate Ordnance Department a total of seventeen bronze 3.3-inch calibre rifled cannon between October 1861 and April 1862. A surviving example with five-groove rifling, weighing 877 pounds, can be found at the Smithsonian Institution, Washington, D.C.

Fig. III A-73
Confederate (copy)
James Pattern I, Sub-pattern I

DIAMETER:	3.25 inches
GUN:	3.3-inch Confederate rifle
LENGTH:	7 9/16 inches
WEIGHT:	10 pounds 1 ounce
CONSTRUCTION:	Solid shot
SABOT:	Lead ring (missing)
FUZING:	None

This is a fired example of the projectile in figure III A-72. Most fired examples of this Confederate copy of the James projectile pattern are found with the lead sabot missing and the ribbed portion of the projectile body broken off. Solid-shot projectiles were intended for use against fortifications such as cannon emplacements. Note the prominent vertical mold seam typical of Confederate manufactured projectiles. Confederate copies of the James projectile pattern have a characteristically rounded nose and distinctly different style of ribs as compared to the original James pattern.

Fig. III A-74
Federal
James Pattern I, Sub-pattern I

Fig. III A-75
Federal
James Pattern I, Sub-pattern I

Fig. III A-76
Federal
James Pattern I, Sub-pattern II

DIAMETER:	3.68 inches
GUN:	14-pounder James rifle, 3.8-inch calibre
LENGTH:	7 inches
WEIGHT:	13 pounds 11 ounces
CONSTRUCTION:	Solid shot
SABOT:	Lead ring covered with a tin sleeve
FUZING:	None

This is a non-excavated, unfired James Pattern I, Sub-pattern I, projectile. The sabot was created by placing a plate of sheet-tin on a piece of strong canvas wider than but of the same length as the plate. The canvas was then folded over the side edges of the sheet-tin plate, secured by cross sewing, and the space between the inner surface of the canvas-covered tin plate and the body of the cylinder filled with melted lead. The canvas was greased prior to the projectile's insertion into the cannon to reduce friction. This pattern was patented by Charles Tillinghast James on February 26, 1856, patent #14,315, and is classified as Pattern I, Sub-pattern I, due to the patent date.

DIAMETER:	3.74 inches
GUN:	14-pounder James rifle, 3.8-inch calibre
LENGTH:	7 inches
WEIGHT:	10 pounds 7 ounces
CONSTRUCTION:	Shell
SABOT:	Lead ring covered with a tin sleeve (missing)
FUZING:	James percussion, brass

Most of the James Pattern I projectiles lost their lead sabot after leaving the cannon. This specimen illustrates the distinctive ribs of the Federal James projectile. When fired over friendly troops, this tendency of the projectile to lose its sabot was found to be unacceptable. Attempts to correct this problem led to the development of the James Pattern II projectile, which was patented on June 10, 1862, patent #35,521. See page 60, figure III A-77, for an example of the James Pattern II projectile. See page 14, figure II A-9, for a cross-section of a James Pattern I, Sub-pattern I, projectile.

DIAMETER:	3.69 inches
GUN:	14-pounder James rifle, 3.8-inch calibre
LENGTH:	7 3/8 inches
WEIGHT:	9 pounds 14 ounces
CONSTRUCTION:	Shell
SABOT:	Lead ring covered with a tin sleeve (missing)
FUZING:	James percussion, brass

This specimen is an example of the James Pattern I, Sub-pattern II, projectile. This sub-pattern is commonly called a tie-ring James due to the visible ring extending below the base of the projectile body. The visible small notches, located in the raised portion of the projectile's ribbed body, were developed in an attempt to improve the chances of the lead sabot remaining attached to the projectile body during firing.

Fig. III A-77
Federal
James Pattern II

Fig. III A-78
Federal
James Pattern II

Fig. III A-79
Federal
James Pattern II

DIAMETER: 3.75 inches
GUN: 14-pounder James rifle, 3.8-inch calibre
LENGTH: 7 3/4 inches
WEIGHT: 16 pounds 14 ounces
CONSTRUCTION: Solid shot
SABOT: Lead with a tin sleeve
FUZING: None

DIAMETER: 3.73 inches
GUN: 14-pounder James rifle, 3.8-inch calibre
LENGTH: 7 3/4 inches
WEIGHT: 12 pounds
CONSTRUCTION: Shell
SABOT: Lead with a tin sleeve (missing)
FUZING: James percussion

DIAMETER: 3.76 inches
GUN: 14-pounder James rifle, 3.8-inch calibre
LENGTH: 7 3/4 inches
WEIGHT: 14 pounds 12 ounces
CONSTRUCTION: Shell
SABOT: Lead with a tin sleeve
FUZING: James percussion

Due to the patent date of June 10, 1862, patent #35,521, this projectile is classified as a James Pattern II projectile. The majority of these projectiles have been recovered from the 1863 Siege of Vicksburg, Mississippi. This James pattern has eight vertical flanges on the projectile body. The sabot is made of lead that has been cast in-between these flanges. The exterior of the sabot is covered with a thin tin sleeve and canvas to help prevent the lead from fouling the bore of the rifled cannon. The fired James Pattern II projectiles are often recovered with the lead sabot intact.

Charles T. James patented this Pattern II projectile on June 10, 1862, patent #35,521. The projectile's body has eight vertical flanges and is tapered in a manner similar to that of a Schenkl. The flanges are wide on the circumference but narrow as they join the shell. The shell version of this pattern is more common than the solid shot. A number of examples have been recovered from the 1863 Siege of Vicksburg, Mississippi. The last ordnance contract for the manufacture of James projectiles was on July 28, 1864.

Note the tin covering on the lead sabot, which was an attempt to help prevent the leading of the cannon bore during firing, which caused excessive wear and tear on the cannon's rifling. The two-piece James percussion fuze often failed to explode the projectile, and even when the fuze worked properly, the small, ineffective bursting cavity often led to unsatisfactory fragmentation. The seam where the tin covering joined together is clearly visible. Note the impression of the canvas on the tin sides of the projectile's sabot. See page 14, figure II A-10, for a cross-section view.

Fig. III A-80
Confederate
Mullane Pattern I, Sub-pattern I

Fig. III A-81
Confederate
Mullane Pattern I, Sub-pattern I

Fig. III A-82
Confederate
Mullane Pattern I, Sub-pattern II

DIAMETER:	2.16 inches
GUN:	Confederate mountain rifle, 2.25-inch calibre
LENGTH:	5 5/8 inches
WEIGHT:	2 pounds 11 ounces
CONSTRUCTION:	Shell
SABOT:	Copper plate
FUZING:	Wooden fuze plug, paper time fuze

DIAMETER:	2.18 inches
GUN:	Confederate mountain rifle, 2.25-inch calibre
LENGTH:	4 5/8 inches
WEIGHT:	2 pounds 11 ounces
CONSTRUCTION:	Shell
SABOT:	Copper plate
FUZING:	Copper fuze plug, paper time fuze

DIAMETER:	2.94 inches
GUN:	3-inch wrought iron (ordnance) rifle
LENGTH:	7 15/16 inches
WEIGHT:	7 pounds 3 ounces
CONSTRUCTION:	Shell
SABOT:	Copper plate
FUZING:	Wooden fuze plug, paper time fuze

This Mullane pattern projectile is sometimes called the Tennessee sabot shell. The Confederate Patent Office refused to issue a patent for the Mullane projectile on the grounds that the design was anticipated by the patent of Dr. John B. Read. This pattern has a characteristic saucer-shaped copper sabot with a wooden dowel pin attached under it to aid in a uniform expansion. A small center bolt held the dowel and sabot in place. This example is missing the wooden dowel. Specimens have been recovered from Augusta, Georgia, and near Selma, Alabama. The bronze Confederate 2.25-inch calibre mountain rifle weighed approximately 200 pounds.

The copper fuze plug shown in this specimen is smaller in diameter than the standard Confederate copper fuze plug used in Read projectiles. The central bolt is flush with the sabot, which is seldom seen in the Mullane pattern. Three iron pins protrude from the base of the projectile through corresponding holes in the copper plate. These iron pins were designed to help prevent the sabot from spinning around the center bolt when fired.

This is the most common Mullane variety recovered in the 3-inch calibre size. It is often found with the copper sabot deformed or missing. An article written in 1866 by Confederate General Edward Porter Alexander, located in the *Southern Historical Society Papers,* states that the Mullane shell "failed, however, about three times out of four times [by] breaking its connection with the copper sabot, and it very frequently exploded in the gun; while of those which flew correctly, not one-fourth exploded at all."

Fig. III A-83
Confederate
Mullane Pattern II, Sub-pattern I

DIAMETER:	2.94 inches
GUN:	3-inch wrought iron (ordnance) rifle
LENGTH:	7 3/4 inches
WEIGHT:	7 pounds 3 ounces
CONSTRUCTION:	Shell
SABOT:	Copper plate
FUZING:	Copper fuze plug, paper time fuze

The typical Mullane projectile in this calibre is found with a wooden fuze plug for a paper time fuze. This specimen was found near the 1864 battlefield of Kennesaw Mountain, Georgia, and has a copper fuze plug. Attempts were made to increase the chances of ignition of the paper time fuze by filing notches in the copper sabot to allow the flame of the discharge to pass. This met with limited success. Note the one flame groove cut out in the copper sabot in this projectile. Approximately one-fourth of the Mullane projectiles that were fired exploded.

Fig. III A-84
Confederate
Mullane Pattern II, Sub-pattern I

DIAMETER:	2.94 inches
GUN:	3-inch wrought iron (ordnance) rifle
LENGTH:	8 3/8 inches
WEIGHT:	7 pounds 4 ounces
CONSTRUCTION:	Case shot
SABOT:	Copper plate
FUZING:	Copper fuze plug, paper time fuze

Mullane side-loader projectiles are extremely rare. The Confederates substituted iron case-shot balls for lead due to the shortage of lead needed for small arms ammunition. The iron balls were inserted through the hole on the projectile's side, and the hot, liquefied matrix was poured into the side-loading hole. Because the Confederates could not drill into the iron balls to form the bursting cavity without great difficulty, the bursting cavity was formed by a dowel inserted into the fuze opening. After the matrix cooled, the dowel was removed, a threaded lead plug screwed into the loading hole, powder installed, and the fuze adapter screwed in.

Fig. III A-85
Confederate
Mullane Pattern II, Sub-pattern I

DIAMETER:	3.45 inches
GUN:	12-pounder Blakely rifle, 3.5-inch calibre
LENGTH:	7 1/4 inches
WEIGHT:	11 pounds 5 ounces
CONSTRUCTION:	Shell
SABOT:	Copper plate
FUZING:	Wooden fuze plug, paper time fuze

The sabot on this projectile has three iron pins that protrude through the copper plate and one center bolt flush with the sabot plate. The Confederates manufactured this pattern for the British 12-pounder (3.5-inch calibre) Blakely rifle in order to keep up with the demand for ammunition, since there was only a limited supply of Britten projectiles imported from Great Britain. Note the impressions of the seven lands and grooves of the Blakely rifle on the copper sabot of this fired projectile.

Read vs. Parrott

Fig. III A-86
Federal
Read-Parrott

Fig. III A-87
Confederate
Read-Parrott

The authors feel that an area of potential confusion exists in the ability to tell the difference between a smooth-sided Confederate Read-Parrott and a Federal Read-Parrott projectile. Base views of both projectiles are shown here for comparison. On the reader's right (Fig. III A-87) is a Confederate manufactured Read-Parrott, which can be identified by the lathe dimple in the base of the projectile body, a thinner wrought iron ring sabot, and lathing marks that run the entire length of the cylindrical body. Although difficult to see in this photograph, the slope, the angle, and the space between the wrought iron ring sabot and bottom of the cylindrical body is slightly different in appearance than that of the Federal projectile on the reader's left (Fig. III A-86). The Federal Read-Parrott projectile exhibits a large chiseled area on the base where the gate waste was removed after casting. Also note there is no evidence of a lathe dimple, since the cylindrical body was not machine-turned. The wrought iron ring is thicker and pre-stamped with corresponding rifling projections (pre-rifled) in all Federal Read-Parrott projectiles; only rarely do Confederate Read-Parrott projectiles exhibit similar pre-stamped projections.

Differences can also be seen when comparing the commonly found fuzes. The Confederate Read-Parrott projectile is most often found with a wooden fuze plug or a copper fuze plug adapter. The Federal Read-Parrott projectile is commonly found with a white metal fuze plug made of zinc.

We hope the above information helps the collector to determine the correct pattern of a questionable projectile. There is, however, no substitute for hands-on experience.

See page 69, figure III A-100, for a Confederate Read-Parrott projectile, and see page 65, figure III A-91, for a Federal Read-Parrott projectile. For more information concerning Read vs. Parrott, see page 68.

Fig. III A-88
Federal
Read-Parrott

Fig. III A-89
Federal
Parrott

Fig. III A-90
Federal
Parrott

DIAMETER:	2.86 inches
GUN:	10-pounder Parrott rifle, 2.9-inch calibre
LENGTH:	6 1/2 inches
WEIGHT:	9 pounds 9 ounces
CONSTRUCTION:	Solid shot
SABOT:	Wrought iron ring
FUZING:	None

DIAMETER:	2.86 inches
GUN:	10-pounder Parrott rifle, 2.9-inch calibre
LENGTH:	6 9/16 inches
WEIGHT:	10 pounds 4 ounces
CONSTRUCTION:	Solid shot
SABOT:	Brass ring
FUZING:	None

DIAMETER:	2.87 inches
GUN:	10-pounder Parrott rifle, 2.9-inch calibre
LENGTH:	6 13/16 inches
WEIGHT:	9 pounds 11 ounces
CONSTRUCTION:	Solid shot
SABOT:	Brass ring
FUZING:	None

Captain Robert Parker Parrott, superintendent of the West Point Gun Foundry, patented this projectile, commonly called a Read-Parrott flat-nose bolt, on August 20, 1861, patent #33,100. Due to the date of introduction into service, Parrott projectiles with the wrought iron ring sabot are classified as Federal Read-Parrott projectiles. This sabot improvement was an attempt to correct the problem that Dr. John B. Read had with his patented thin wrought iron ring projectile. Parrott's improvement was a thicker wrought iron ring with three corresponding rifling projections (pre-rifling) stamped into the sabot. This helped to prevent the breakage of the wrought iron ring during expansion.

This Parrott flat-nose bolt was found in Vicksburg, Mississippi. The Parrott rifles of 3-inch calibre were not delivered to the Federal army until February of 1864. The siege of Vicksburg ended on July 4, 1863; thus all 10-pounder Parrott projectiles with brass and iron sabots found on battlefields prior to February 1864 were fired from the 10-pounder Parrott rifles of 2.9-inch calibre. This type of brass sabot was cast on the projectile after the cast iron body was removed from the mold.

The majority of battlefield recoveries of this variety of 10-pounder (2.9-inch calibre) Parrott chilled-nose bolt projectile have been at Vicksburg, Mississippi. The purpose of this bolt was to punch through fortifications, buildings, and other structures. The thick brass sabot was cast flush with the bottom of the iron base with no gap or space for the expansion gases to enter. The sabot often failed to enter the grooves of the cannon rifling, thus affecting the range and accuracy of the fired projectile. This style of projectile is also found in a 20-pounder (3.67-inch calibre) size.

Fig. III A-91
Federal
Read-Parrott

DIAMETER:	2.86 inches
GUN:	10-pounder Parrott rifle, 2.9-inch calibre
LENGTH:	8 7/8 inches
WEIGHT:	8 pounds 15 ounces
CONSTRUCTION:	Shell
SABOT:	Wrought iron ring
FUZING:	Parrott percussion, zinc

All Federal Read-Parrott projectiles with wrought iron ring sabots were manufactured for use in the 10-pounder Parrott rifle of 2.9-inch calibre. The wrought iron ring was made first and placed into the projectile mold so that it was firmly embedded in the metal body. The projectile was then placed in a metal cylinder and pre-stamped (according to Parrott's patent information) with the rifling grooves. The fuze consists of a zinc anvil cap and a zinc striker. A percussion cap rested upon the iron nipple of the zinc striker. Upon firing, the striker often bound at an angle inside the threaded fuze cavity of the projectile's nose, thus preventing detonation due to lack of contact with the anvil cap.

Fig. III A-92
Federal
Parrott

DIAMETER:	2.94 inches
GUN:	3-inch Parrott rifle
LENGTH:	8 7/8 inches
WEIGHT:	11 pounds 11 ounces
CONSTRUCTION:	Case shot
SABOT:	Brass ring
FUZING:	Parrott zinc fuze plug, paper time fuze

Parrott patented this projectile's sabot construction on August 20, 1861, patent #33,099. The high brass sabot ring was cast around the base of the projectile, which had six indentations. The purpose of these indentations was to help keep the sabot from slipping while the propellant charge forced the sabot into the grooves of the rifle. Most often the sabot would not enter the grooves of the rifle cannon upon firing due to the close tolerance between the sabot and the shell base. Occasionally this resulted in chipping of the iron base of the projectile. Many field recoveries have had the sabot sawed with vertical lines to correct the expansion problems.

Fig. III A-93
Federal
Parrott

DIAMETER:	2.86 inches
GUN:	10-pounder Parrott rifle, 2.9-inch calibre
LENGTH:	8 9/16 inches
WEIGHT:	10 pounds 2 ounces
CONSTRUCTION:	Case shot
SABOT:	Brass ring
FUZING:	Parrott zinc fuze plug, paper time fuze

In order to correct the chipping problem of the sabot type in figure III A-92, the sabot shown here was developed with five internal flanges. However, this caused the bottom of the sabot to be flush with the base of the shell which, in combination with the extreme thickness of the sabot, would not allow the explosive charge to force the sabot into the grooves of the gun tube. Often the shells failed to take the rifling of the bore, thereby decreasing their range and accuracy. The projectile body was cast and sized with a die while hot. The brass ring was cast on the projectile's base afterward. See page 15, figure II A-11, for a cross-section view.

Fig. III A-94
Federal
Parrott

Fig. III A-95
Federal
Read-Parrott

Fig. III A-96
Federal
Parrott

DIAMETER:	3.63 inches
GUN:	20-pounder Parrott rifle, 3.67-inch calibre
LENGTH:	8 7/8 inches
WEIGHT:	19 pounds 14 ounces
CONSTRUCTION:	Solid shot
SABOT:	Brass ring
FUZING:	None

DIAMETER:	3.63 inches
GUN:	20-pounder Parrott rifle, 3.67-inch calibre
LENGTH:	9 1/4 inches
WEIGHT:	17 pounds 15 ounces
CONSTRUCTION:	Case shot
SABOT:	Wrought iron ring
FUZING:	Parrott zinc fuze plug, paper time fuze

DIAMETER:	3.63 inches
GUN:	20-pounder Parrott rifle, 3.67-inch calibre
LENGTH:	10 1/8 inches
WEIGHT:	18 pounds 1 ounce
CONSTRUCTION:	Shell
SABOT:	Brass ring
FUZING:	Parrott zinc fuze plug, paper time fuze

This style of Parrott projectile is commonly referred to as a Parrott chilled-nose bolt. An explanation of the manufacturing process for this projectile's nose can be found in the chilled-iron definition in our glossary. This projectile was designed primarily for destroying fortifications and was not used as an anti-personnel projectile. It is also found in a 10-pounder (2.9-inch calibre) size. Note the expanded brass sabot on this fired example which shows the impressions of the five lands and grooves from the 20-pounder (3.67-inch calibre) Parrott rifle.

Typically, the short variety of the 20-pounder (3.67-inch calibre) Read-Parrott shell was filled with lead case-shot balls. Due to the added weight of the case-shot material, the projectile was shortened to keep the weight under 20 pounds. The wrought iron sabot ring was suspended in a mold around which the iron body was poured, thus embedding the sabot during this casting process. This was unlike the later production brass Parrott sabots, which were cast directly onto the body. Parrott patented an improvement upon Read's sabot design; therefore, the name Read-Parrott is assigned to all Federal and Confederate projectiles with this iron sabot style and body design.

This is an example of the long-pattern 20-pounder (3.67-inch calibre) Parrott projectile. Typically, the long-pattern Parrott projectiles are common shell and not case-shot. A large number of this style of projectile were fired during the 1864 Atlanta Campaign. This pattern is also found with a wrought iron ring sabot; in those cases, it is considered a Read-Parrott projectile.

Fig. III A-97
Confederate Read

Fig. III A-98
Confederate Read

DIAMETER:	2.94 inches
GUN:	3-inch wrought iron (ordnance) rifle
LENGTH:	6 1/4 inches
WEIGHT:	8 pounds 1 ounces
CONSTRUCTION:	Solid shot
SABOT:	Copper ring
FUZING:	None

DIAMETER:	2.94 inches
GUN:	3-inch Confederate rifle
LENGTH:	6 1/4 inches
WEIGHT:	8 pounds
CONSTRUCTION:	Solid shot
SABOT:	Copper ring
FUZING:	None

This pattern is the most commonly recovered 3-inch Read bolt projectile. Most specimens have been recovered from Snyder's Bluff, Mississippi. Note that the copper sabot is thick and unevenly cast, which is typical of the occasionally rushed Confederate manufacture. A few projectiles of this pattern have been recovered from the 1864 Resaca, Georgia, battlefield north of Atlanta.

This projectile's nose is more pointed and the copper sabot taller and thinner than that shown in figure III A-97. Note the well-defined pattern of the twelve lands and grooves of the 3-inch Confederate rifle impressed on the copper sabot while firing. This specimen was fired by the Federal artillery with captured Confederate cannon and ammunition during the 1863 Siege of Vicksburg, Mississippi. The range of the Confederate 3-inch rifle at 6° elevation was 2,250 yards.

Fig. III A-99
Federal
Read-Parrott

DIAMETER:	2.87 inches
GUN:	10-pounder Parrott rifle, 2.9-inch calibre
LENGTH:	8 3/4 inches
WEIGHT:	8 pounds 14 ounces
CONSTRUCTION:	Shell
SABOT:	Wrought iron ring
FUZING:	Wooden fuze plug, paper time fuze

Robert P. Parrott and Dr. John B. Read were both projectile inventors before the Civil War. Read patented his wrought iron ring sabot projectiles on October 28, 1856, patent #15,999. Parrott purchased from Read the rights to manufacture Read's projectile before 1861, and a royalty was to be paid to Dr. Read. On August 20, 1861, with patent #33,100, Parrott patented an improvement upon Read's projectiles. Parrott's patent stated, in part: "This invention consists in an improvement upon the elongated projectile for which letters Patent of the United States were issued on the 28th day of October, 1856, to John B. Read....the cups [Read ring sabots] became so weak as to be liable to break away from the body of the projectile....to prevent this, I make the said cup, more especially at its edges, of greater thickness, and to insure its proper entrance into the grooves I swage or otherwise form the said cup before the insertion of the projectile in the gun in such a manner that in loading it will enter into the grooves in such a manner that if will not interfere with the free loading of the gun, but that in loading it will be driven completely into the grooves and caused to fit the grooves and lands by the force of the explosion of the charge of powder without any danger of its being broken."

According to a letter written by Parrott, this projectile pattern was tested at the Washington Arsenal under the command of Brigadier General George D. Ramsay in June 1861 and was used exclusively by Ricketts' Battery at First Manassas. The projectile shown here, which was recovered from the site of the Battle of First Manassas, is exactly like that drawn and described in Parrott's patent #33,100. Although the projectile is of Federal manufacture, the sabot design falls under Read's patent of October 28, 1856; Parrott only made an improvement upon Read's wrought iron ring sabot. Therefore, all wrought iron ring sabot projectiles similar to this example should be classified as the Read-Parrott pattern. Parrott later patented a brass ring sabot which should properly be referred to by his name only. The later Parrott patterns have been threaded for fuzes and have brass sabots.

Fig. III A-100
Confederate Read-Parrott

DIAMETER:	2.87 inches
GUN:	10-pounder Parrott rifle, 2.9-inch calibre
LENGTH:	9 inches
WEIGHT:	10 pounds
CONSTRUCTION:	Shell
SABOT:	Wrought iron ring
FUZING:	Wooden fuze plug, paper time fuze

This is an example of the combination of Read's wrought iron sabot and Parrott's body design. This projectile was used primarily in the 10-pounder (2.9-inch calibre) Parrott rifle. Confederate projectiles with this body style should be properly referred to as Read-Parrott's. Stamped on opposite sides of the body are the letters "AR," possibly the stamp of A.J. Rahm, proprietor of Eagle Machine Works in Richmond, Virginia. His company manufactured artillery, artillery carriages, ammunition and tools, and outfitted gunboats from 1862 to 1864. Several Read-Parrott specimens with the "AR" stamp have been recovered from sites in Virginia and South Carolina.

Fig. III A-101
Confederate Read-Parrott

DIAMETER:	2.85 inches
GUN:	10-pounder Parrott rifle, 2.9-inch calibre
LENGTH:	9 1/4 inches
WEIGHT:	9 pounds 15 ounces
CONSTRUCTION:	Shell
SABOT:	Wrought iron ring
FUZING:	Copper fuze plug, paper time fuze

Smooth-sided Read-Parrott projectiles were first manufactured with a tapered fuze-well that took a wooden fuze plug. The copper fuze plug in this example indicates later production. Confederate Read-Parrott projectiles with a smooth-sided appearance continued until difficulties in production led to the development of bourrelets, which sped up manufacturing by saving on tooling time. Several foundries, including the Atlanta Arsenal, were able to manufacture the smooth-sided pattern throughout the war. The surface of the projectile parallel to the sides of the bore had to be machined to the required dimension to allow for windage.

Fig. III A-102
Confederate Read-Parrott

DIAMETER:	2.86 inches
GUN:	10-pounder Parrott rifle, 2.9-inch calibre
LENGTH:	8 3/4 inches
WEIGHT:	8 pounds 6 ounces
CONSTRUCTION:	Shell
SABOT:	Wrought iron ring
FUZING:	Copper fuze plug, paper time fuze

This projectile has two bourrelets, or bearing surfaces, with the upper bourrelet having a greater width than the lower. The bottom bourrelet has been machined down to the diameter of the projectile body. The projectile base is slightly rounded with a lathe dimple, and the sabot is made of thin wrought iron. This Read-Parrott was most likely manufactured at Tredegar Iron Works in Richmond, Virginia. See page 16, figure II A-13, for a representative cross-section view.

Fig. III A-103
Confederate
Read-Parrott

DIAMETER:	2.85 inches
GUN:	10-pounder Parrott rifle, 2.9-inch calibre
LENGTH:	8 1/2 inches
WEIGHT:	10 pounds 1 ounce
CONSTRUCTION:	Case shot
SABOT:	Wrought iron ring
FUZING:	Copper fuze plug, paper time fuze

Note the chipping around the projectile base, which was due to the poor iron and sabot design used by the Confederates. Located near the base is a rebated section developed by the Confederates in an attempt to decrease the extent of chipping, which was often severe in projectiles of this style. See page 72, figure III A-110, for an example of severe chipping. This projectile contains iron case-shot balls that were inserted through the side-loading hole, which is now closed with a lead plug. This Confederate-pattern Read-Parrott projectile is scarce. The pictured specimen was recovered from the 1863 Siege of Vicksburg, Mississippi. See figure III A-104 for a description of the method of case-shot manufacture.

Fig. III A-104
Confederate
Read

DIAMETER:	2.96 inches
GUN:	3-inch wrought iron (ordnance) rifle
LENGTH:	7 5/16 inches
WEIGHT:	8 pounds 14 ounces
CONSTRUCTION:	Case shot
SABOT:	Copper ring
FUZING:	Copper fuze plug, paper time fuze

Because the Confederates desperately needed lead for small arms ammunition, they substituted iron for lead when manufacturing case-shot balls. This substitution presented a difficult situation, as they could not drill into the iron balls to form the bursting cavity without damaging the drill bits or breaking the matrix loose. To circumvent this problem, the bursting cavity was formed by inserting a dowel into the fuze opening. The iron balls were inserted through the hole on the projectile's side, and the hot, liquefied matrix was poured into the side-loading hole. After the matrix cooled, the dowel was removed, a lead plug screwed into the loading hole, powder installed, and the fuze adapter screwed into the nose of the projectile. Side-loading rifled case-shot projectiles are rare. The example pictured has three frame grooves cut into the sabot, a lathe dog near the top of the nose, and a lathe dimple in the base. It is loaded with iron case-shot balls.

Fig. III A-105
Confederate
Read-Parrott

DIAMETER:	2.85 inches
GUN:	10-pounder Parrott rifle, 2.9-inch calibre
LENGTH:	8 5/8 inches
WEIGHT:	10 pounds 2 ounces
CONSTRUCTION:	Shell
SABOT:	Copper ring
FUZING:	Wooden fuze plug, paper time fuze

This is an example of a Read-Parrott pattern projectile with a high, thin copper sabot. Most specimens of this pattern have been recovered from battlefields near Atlanta, Georgia, such as the 1864 Battle of Kennesaw Mountain. The projectile base has a lathe dimple and is slightly rounded. This style of Read-Parrott was manufactured at the Atlanta Arsenal in Atlanta, Georgia. This projectile was manufactured for use in the 10-pounder (2.9-inch calibre) Parrott rifle, which at an elevation of 15° had a flight time of 16 seconds and a range of 4,100 yards.

Fig. III A-106
Confederate
Read-Parrott

DIAMETER:	2.93 inches
GUN:	3-inch Parrott rifle
LENGTH:	7 5/8 inches
WEIGHT:	8 pounds
CONSTRUCTION:	Shell
SABOT:	Copper ring
FUZING:	Wooden fuze plug, paper time fuze

This style of Read-Parrott projectile is often referred to as a Trans-Mississippi Read-Parrott due to the fact that all examples of this pattern have been recovered from Western Theater sites. Three flame grooves were cut out of the thin copper sabot to help increase the likelihood of the propellant flame reaching the paper time fuze. Examples of this style are also found in 2.25-inch, 3.3-inch and 3.5-inch calibres.

Fig. III A-107
Confederate
Read-Parrott

DIAMETER:	2.84 inches
GUN:	10-pounder Parrott rifle, 2.9-inch calibre
LENGTH:	8 1/2 inches
WEIGHT:	9 pounds 8 ounces
CONSTRUCTION:	Shell
SABOT:	Copper ring
FUZING:	Copper fuze plug, paper time fuze

This Read-Parrott pattern is usually recovered from Atlanta Campaign Battlefields such as the 1864 Battle of Kolb's Farm, Georgia. Projectiles of this style were manufactured at the Atlanta Arsenal. The projectile base, hidden by the very thick, brittle copper sabot, is rounded. Note the one flame groove notch cut into the copper sabot. Fired specimens that have been recovered are usually found with most of the sabot missing.

Fig. III A-108
Confederate Read

Fig. III A-109
Confederate Read

Fig. III A-110
Confederate Read

DIAMETER:	2.94 inches
GUN:	3-inch wrought iron (ordnance) rifle
LENGTH:	7 5/16 inches
WEIGHT:	8 pounds
CONSTRUCTION:	Shell
SABOT:	Copper ring
FUZING:	Wooden fuze plug, paper time fuze

This particular Read pattern was developed to save man hours and tooling costs. Instead of having to turn the entire length of the projectile body on a lathe, only the two bourrelets needed to be machined to tolerance. This projectile is an example of an early bourreleted Read pattern manufactured for a wooden fuze plug. Note the distinct mold seam running the entire length of the projectile body. The copper sabot shows excellent rifling impressions from the 3-inch rifle wrought iron (ordnance) rifle.

DIAMETER:	2.96 inches
GUN:	3-inch wrought iron (ordnance) rifle
LENGTH:	7 1/2 inches
WEIGHT:	6 pounds 4 ounces
CONSTRUCTION:	Shell
SABOT:	Copper ring
FUZING:	Copper fuze plug, paper time fuze

This is the most commonly recovered Read pattern projectile. This specimen is unfired. A lathe dimple is found in the center of the projectile base. This pattern of Read was designed to be fired from the 3-inch wrought iron (ordnance) rifle having seven lands and grooves. This specimen is located in the West Point Military Academy Museum, West Point, New York. Note the original leather washer underneath the copper fuze plug. The leather washer helped seal the fuze plug against any bypass of the propellant charge. See page 16, figure II A-14, for a cross-section view of a projectile of this pattern.

DIAMETER:	2.93 inches
GUN:	3-inch wrought iron (ordnance) rifle
LENGTH:	7 1/2 inches
WEIGHT:	N/A, chipped iron base
CONSTRUCTION:	Shell
SABOT:	Copper ring
FUZING:	Copper fuze plug (missing), paper time fuze

The poor quality of iron used in the Confederate-manufactured projectiles is evident in this specimen. When the sabot was forced into the grooves of the rifle during firing, the expansion often broke the iron around the base of the projectile. Due to this chipping problem, Dr. Read developed a groove to allow the sabot room for forward displacement during expansion. This groove between the sabot and the iron body is known as the "Read safety groove." Note the impression of the seven lands and grooves from the 3-inch wrought iron (ordnance) rifle on the copper sabot. This specimen is located in the West Point Military Academy Museum.

Fig. III A-III
Confederate
Read

Fig. III A-II2
Confederate
Read

Fig. III A-II3
Confederate
Read

DIAMETER:	3.22 inches
GUN:	3.3-inch Confederate rifle
LENGTH:	5 3/4 inches
WEIGHT:	8 pounds 11 ounces
CONSTRUCTION:	Solid shot
SABOT:	Copper ring
FUZING:	None

DIAMETER:	3.23 inches
GUN:	3.3-inch Confederate rifle
LENGTH:	6 15/16 inches
WEIGHT:	8 pounds 14 ounces
CONSTRUCTION:	Shell
SABOT:	Copper ring
FUZING:	Copper fuze plug, paper time fuze

DIAMETER:	3.22 inches
GUN:	3.3-inch Confederate rifle
LENGTH:	6 7/8 inches
WEIGHT:	8 pounds 1 ounce
CONSTRUCTION:	Shell
SABOT:	Copper ring
FUZING:	Confederate percussion, copper anvil cap

This style of Read bolt was manufactured at the Selma Arsenal in Selma, Alabama, and was intended for used in the 3.3-inch Confederate rifled cannon. An example of a 3.3-inch Confederate rifled cannon is located in the Museum of the Confederacy in Richmond, Virginia. Note the two wide bourrelets and the high copper sabot on this pictured example. This variety of Read has been recovered from Selma, Alabama; Milledgeville, Georgia; and Shiloh, Tennessee.

The Official Records, Series I, Volume XLIV, report number 90 of Colonel William Hawley, 3rd Wisconsin Infantry, states that on or around November 22, 1864, Hawley's troops threw 170 boxes of fixed artillery ammunition into the Oconee River at Milledgeville (the wartime capital of Georgia) and also destroyed the weapons that the Confederates had stored in Milledgeville. As similar specimens of all patterns on this page have been recovered from the Selma Arsenal site, it may be assumed that they were also manufactured there. This rare unfired Read projectile has a high copper sabot with one flame groove. This projectile was recovered from Milledgeville, Georgia.

Note the high-band sabot usually found on this Read pattern. This Read projectile was manufactured at the Selma Arsenal in Alabama and was recovered from Milledgeville, Georgia. At least one specimen was recovered from the 1862 Shiloh Battlefield in Tennessee where Watson's Louisiana Battery had four rifles of this calibre engaged.

Fig. III A-114
Confederate
Read-Parrott

Fig. III A-115
Confederate
Read-Parrott

Fig. III A-116
Confederate
Read-Parrott

DIAMETER:	3.34 inches
GUN:	3.4-inch rifle
LENGTH:	6 1/4 inches
WEIGHT:	8 pounds 1 ounce
CONSTRUCTION:	Shell
SABOT:	Wrought iron ring
FUZING:	Wooden fuze plug, paper time fuze

DIAMETER:	3.35 inches
GUN:	3.4-inch calibre rifle
LENGTH:	7 7/8 inches
WEIGHT:	11 pounds 7 ounces
CONSTRUCTION:	Shell
SABOT:	Copper ring
FUZING:	Copper fuze plug, paper time fuze

DIAMETER:	3.44 inches
GUN:	12-pounder Blakely rifle, 3.5-inch calibre
LENGTH:	7 1/8 inches
WEIGHT:	11 pounds 13 ounces
CONSTRUCTION:	Shell
SABOT:	Copper ring
FUZING:	Wooden fuze plug, paper time fuze

Note the distinctly visible lathe grooves running the entire length of this cylindrical Read-Parrott projectile body. The wrought iron sabot has the impression of three lands and grooves stamped into it. This was done in an attempt to decrease the likelihood of the sabot breaking as it expanded into the grooves of the rifle during firing. For more information concerning the construction of pre-stamped wrought iron ring sabots see page 68. Because the basic body design of this projectile is smooth-sided and without bourrelets, the authors have decided to classify it as a Read-Parrott even though this projectile was not manufactured for use in the Parrott rifle.

This unfired Read-Parrott specimen was recovered from a Confederate Fort located at High Bridge, Virginia. Several hundred projectiles of various patterns were found in this cache. This example has a time fuze plug made of copper. The 4-pounder smoothbore cannon were originally cast at the Virginia Manufactory of Arms in the early 1800s and were subsequently rifled to 3.4-inch calibre by the Confederates during the war.

The Federal Naval Blockade slowed and often prevented the Confederates from receiving Britten projectiles from Great Britain. This Confederate-manufactured Read-Parrott projectile pattern was developed in an attempt to replace the difficult-to-obtain Britten projectiles. Notice the lathe dog near the fuze hole of the projectile. The excellent seven lands and grooves pattern of the 12-pounder (3.5-inch calibre) Blakely rifle is clearly evident on the thick copper sabot. See page 50, figure III A-52, for an example of the Britten projectile.

Fig. III A-117
Federal
Sawyer

DIAMETER: 3.56 inches
GUN: 6-pounder Sawyer rifle, 3.67-inch calibre
LENGTH: 7 1/8 inches
WEIGHT: 15 pounds 10 ounces
CONSTRUCTION: Solid shot
SABOT: Lead jacket
FUZING: None

Sylvanus Sawyer of Fitchburg, Massachusetts, patented this style of projectile on November 13, 1855, United States patent #13,799. The patent date "Nov. 13, 1855" is stamped on the slightly concave lead base. Note the nice pattern of lands and grooves on the lead sabot from the 3.67-inch Sawyer rifled cannon. This specimen was found at Port Hudson, as have been most examples of this type.

Fig. III A-118
Federal
Sawyer

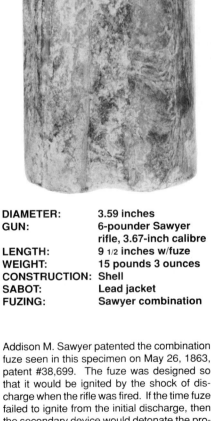

DIAMETER: 3.59 inches
GUN: 6-pounder Sawyer rifle, 3.67-inch calibre
LENGTH: 9 1/2 inches w/fuze
WEIGHT: 15 pounds 3 ounces
CONSTRUCTION: Shell
SABOT: Lead jacket
FUZING: Sawyer combination

Addison M. Sawyer patented the combination fuze seen in this specimen on May 26, 1863, patent #38,699. The fuze was designed so that it would be ignited by the shock of discharge when the rifle was fired. If the time fuze failed to ignite from the initial discharge, then the secondary device would detonate the projectile on impact. This style of fuze is commonly referred to as a Sawyer candlestick fuze. Stamped on the nose is "14 1/2," which is the amount of bursting charge in ounces that was to be installed at the arsenal. Several 3-inch Sawyer projectiles similar to this specimen have been recovered from a Virginia battlefield.

Fig. III A-119
Federal
Sawyer

DIAMETER: 3.61 inches (3.83 across flanges)
GUN: 6-pounder Sawyer rifle, 3.67-inch calibre
LENGTH: 7 5/16 inches
WEIGHT: 12 pounds 4 ounces
CONSTRUCTION: Shell
SABOT: Iron flanges covered with lead jacket
FUZING: Sawyer percussion

Sylvanus Sawyer also patented this fuze on November 13, 1855, patent #13,799. Sawyer shells had poor battlefield performance because the lead jacket expanded when the shell burst, thereby absorbing the shock and not allowing the iron projectile body to fragment properly. This Sawyer pattern has six iron flanges under the lead covering that correspond with the rifling of the cannon bore. The patent date is stamped on the flat base, and stamped on the nose is "11 1/2." This let the factory worker know how many ounces (11 1/2) of bursting charge to load. Most recovered specimens were fired by Holcomb's Vermont Battery during the Siege of Port Hudson, Louisiana.

Fig. III A-120
Federal
Schenkl

DIAMETER:	2.92 inches
GUN:	3-inch wrought iron (ordnance) rifle
LENGTH:	9 3/16 inches
WEIGHT:	8 pounds
CONSTRUCTION:	Shell
SABOT:	Papier-mâché
FUZING:	Schenkl percussion, brass

This was the most common Schenkl pattern purchased by the Federal Ordnance Department. There are seven raised verticle ribs on the tapered cone. Stamped on the brass percussion fuze is "J.P. SCHENKL PAT. OCT. 16, 1861." The actual patent date was October 15, 1861, patent #34,495. According to Abbot's *Siege Artillery in the Campaigns Against Richmond,* the Schenkl percussion fuze was 82% effective. See page 17, figure II A-15, for a cross-section of the 3-inch Schenkl common shell projectile.

Fig. III A-121
Federal
Schenkl

DIAMETER:	2.90 inches
GUN:	3-inch wrought iron (ordnance) rifle
LENGTH:	10 1/8 inches
WEIGHT:	8 pounds w/o sabot
CONSTRUCTION:	Case shot
SABOT:	Papier-mâché
FUZING:	Schenkl combination

The rounded nose on this pattern indicates it is case-shot. Please note the original papier-mâché sabot on this non-excavated example. The lower zinc band, which helped decrease humidity-related swelling, is missing. Because the papier-mâché sabot fit so tightly in the bore, no flame could pass to light the conventional time fuze. A self-igniting fuze was used in an attempt to correct this problem. However, this combination fuze worked poorly, with only an approximate 55% success rate. This shell has seven raised ribs on the tapered cone. See page 22 for the Schenkl combination fuze and page 17, figure A-16, for a cross-section of a 3-inch Schenkl case-shot projectile.

Fig. III A-122
Federal converted to Confederate
Schenkl

DIAMETER:	2.93 inches
GUN:	3-inch rifle
LENGTH:	9 inches
WEIGHT:	8 pounds 2 ounces
CONSTRUCTION:	Shell
SABOT:	Wooden cone (missing)
FUZING:	Confederate copper fuze plug, paper time fuze

This Federal Schenkl was captured by the Confederates and sent to an arsenal where the original papier-mâché sabot was replaced with one made of wood. The Confederates did not have the capability for manufacturing the papier-mâché sabot. The purpose of the iron pin seen at the base of the projectile was to help secure the wooden sabot onto the tapered cone. The original Schenkl brass percussion fuze has been replaced with a Confederate copper time fuze plug.

Fig. III A-123
Federal
Schenkl

DIAMETER:	3.61 inches
GUN:	3.67-inch rifle
LENGTH:	8 1/8 inches
WEIGHT:	10 pounds 7 ounces
CONSTRUCTION:	Shell
SABOT:	Papier-mâché (missing)
FUZING:	Schenkl percussion, brass, unmarked

The tapered portion of the body of this specimen has an unusually shaped cylindrical base knob. Examples of this variety have been recovered from Port Hudson, Louisiana, and Vicksburg, Mississippi. This variety of Schenkl pattern projectile is very rare. This would appear to be an early Schenkl pattern that was manufactured in limited quantities.

Fig. III A-124
Federal
Schenkl

DIAMETER:	3.62 inches
GUN:	3.67-inch calibre rifle
LENGTH:	8 11/16 inches
WEIGHT:	10 pounds 11 ounces
CONSTRUCTION:	Shell
SABOT:	Papier-mâché (missing)
FUZING:	Schenkl percussion, brass

Note that the tapered cone portion of this projectile's body has six recessed areas. Most Schenkl patterns have raised ribs on the tapered cone section. This shell is equipped with a Schenkl brass percussion fuze; specimens have also been recovered with the Schenkl combination fuze. Examples of this pattern have been recovered from Nashville and Port Hudson. In *Siege Artillery in the Campaigns Against Richmond,* Abbot stated: "When the sabot is well made and in good order, this is excellent ammunition. It has a smoother and more silent flight than the Parrott, it gives excellent practice, and the light sabot does not endanger troops in front."

Fig. III A-125
Federal
Schenkl

DIAMETER:	3.55 inches
GUN:	3.67-inch calibre rifle
LENGTH:	8 13/16 inches
WEIGHT:	10 pounds 5 ounces
CONSTRUCTION:	Shell
SABOT:	Papier-mâché (missing)
FUZING:	Schenkl percussion, brass

This specimen has six narrow ribs on the tapered cone portion of the projectile body. The brass Schenkl percussion fuze was patented by John P. Schenkl on October 15, 1861, patent #33,495. However, stamped on this specimen's fuze is "J.P. SCHENKL PAT. OCT. 16, 1861." An improved model was patented by John P. Schenkl on August 19, 1862, patent #36,236.

Fig. III A-126
Confederate
Schenkl copy

DIAMETER:	3.63 inches
GUN:	3.67-inch calibre rifle
LENGTH:	8 1/2 inches
WEIGHT:	13 pounds 7 ounces
CONSTRUCTION:	Solid shot
SABOT:	Wooden cone
FUZING:	None

This specimen represents a Confederate attempt to copy the Schenkl projectile pattern and is believed to have been manufactured at the site of the Marshall Powder Mill in Texas. There are twelve thin raised ribs on the tapered cone portion of the projectile body. The wooden sabot was held on by a thin iron plate. The Confederates lacked the formula for the manufacture of papier-mâché and substituted wood in its place.

Fig. III A-127
Confederate
Schenkl copy

DIAMETER:	3.59 inches
GUN:	3.67-inch calibre rifle
LENGTH:	8 1/4 inches
WEIGHT:	9 pounds 10 ounces
CONSTRUCTION:	Shell
SABOT:	Wooden cone
FUZING:	Wooden fuze plug, paper time fuze

Note the iron plate with its remnants of tin, which originally extended across the base of the wooden sabot and helped to secure it to the tapered cone of the projectile body. This is the shell version of the example in figure III A-126, and the same remarks apply. The bulk of the recovered Confederate Schenkl copies were found where a caisson tumbled off a bridge at the Double Bridges site on Old Texas Star Road near Robeline, Louisiana, during Banks' Red River Campaign. Several were found a mile away near the Welch's Cemetery.

Fig. III A-128
Confederate
Schenkl copy

DIAMETER:	3.71 inches
GUN:	3.8-inch calibre rifle
LENGTH:	8 11/16 inches
WEIGHT:	13 pounds
CONSTRUCTION:	Solid shot
SABOT:	Wooden cone
FUZING:	None

The wooden sabot used by the Confederates in place of papier-mâché is missing. This Confederate copy of the Federal Schenkl pattern has twelve distinct raised ribs on the tapered cone portion of the projectile body. This specimen was recovered from the same site as the projectile in figure III A-126. Note that this variety was manufactured without a pin and the tin plate sabot attachment system that aided in securing the wooden sabot in place.

Fig. III A-129
Confederate
Selma

DIAMETER:	2.43 inches
GUN:	2.5-inch Blakely rifle
LENGTH:	7 1/4 inches
WEIGHT:	5 pounds 14 ounces
CONSTRUCTION:	Shell
SABOT:	Copper plate
FUZING:	Wooden fuze plug, paper time fuze

Projectiles of this pattern are traditionally named after their attributed site of manufacture: the Selma Arsenal in Selma, Alabama. In the groove between the high copper sabot and the cylindrical portion of the projectile body can been seen remnants of a hemp-like material. This material was originally greased, thus helping to serve as a lubricant for the cannon bore. This Selma pattern projectile has a copper sabot that was embedded in the iron body of the projectile during casting by means of a square or rectangle post. Examples of this Selma pattern projectile are extremely rare.

Fig. III A-130
Confederate
Selma

DIAMETER:	2.95 inches
GUN:	3-inch rifle
LENGTH:	7 5/8 inches
WEIGHT:	8 pounds 8 ounces
CONSTRUCTION:	Shell
SABOT:	Copper plate
FUZING:	Wooden fuze plug, paper time fuze

Note the wide lubrication groove between the high copper sabot and the distinct bottom bourrelet of the projectile body. Remnants of the lathe dog can be seen on the projectile's nose. A lathe dimple is found in the center of the copper base. This Selma pattern projectile in this calibre is extremely rare. Most Selma patterns similar to the above specimen have been recovered with the wooden fuze plug missing.

Fig. III A-131
Confederate
Selma

DIAMETER:	3.62 inches
GUN:	20-pounder Parrott rifle, 3.67-inch calibre
LENGTH:	8 15/16 inches
WEIGHT:	16 pounds 6 ounces
CONSTRUCTION:	Shell, lines of weakness
SABOT:	Copper plate
FUZING:	Wooden fuze plug, paper time fuze

This Selma Arsenal-manufactured projectile has lines of weakness cast into the interior of the body in the form of a six-sided prism. Upon successful detonation, these lines of weakness were ideally designed to break the shell into several equal-size fragments, except for the nose and the base. This extremely rare specimen is unfired. A few unfired specimens have been recovered from South Carolina.

Fig. III A-132
Confederate Selma

Fig. III A-133
Confederate Selma

Fig. III A-134
Confederate Selma

DIAMETER:	3.21 inches
GUN:	3.3-inch Confederate rifle
LENGTH:	6 3/4 inches
WEIGHT:	10 pounds 11 ounces
CONSTRUCTION:	Solid shot
SABOT:	Copper plate
FUZING:	None

DIAMETER:	3.26 inches
GUN:	3.3-inch Confederate rifle
LENGTH:	6 13/16 inches
WEIGHT:	11 pounds 7 ounces
CONSTRUCTION:	Solid shot
SABOT:	Copper plate
FUZING:	None

DIAMETER:	3.60 inches
GUN:	3.67-inch calibre rifle
LENGTH:	5 11/16 inches
WEIGHT:	10 pounds 6 ounces
CONSTRUCTION:	Solid shot
SABOT:	Copper plate
FUZING:	None

Stamped into the nose of this projectile and into the bottom of the copper sabot is the letter "G," which indicates Selma Arsenal manufacture. Similar projectiles have been recovered with the letter "R" stamped into the nose and sabot of the projectile. The significance of this letter "R" is unknown to the authors. Numbers are often stamped into the upper bourrelet in similar pattern projectiles, as in figure III A-133. Projectiles of this sub-pattern have been recovered from Milledgeville, Georgia, and Selma, Alabama. The base of the solid copper sabot plate is slightly concave, as is typical of this projectile's sabot system.

This specimen has a more rounded nose than the specimen on the left, and there are fewer examples known of this variety. This projectile was recovered from Milledgeville, Georgia. *The Official Records,* Series I, Volume XLIV, Report number 90 of Colonel William Hawley, 3rd Wisconsin Infantry, states that on or around November 22, 1864, Hawley's troops threw 170 boxes of fixed artillery ammunition into the Oconee River at Milledgeville (the capital of Georgia during the war) and also destroyed the weapons that the Confederates had stored in Milledgeville. The letter "G" is stamped into the nose and copper sabot, and the number "22" is stamped into the upper bourrelet.

Note the heavy lathe marks on the bourrelets as well as the copper sabot of this Selma-manufactured projectile. Most often, fired projectiles in this pattern have the sabot distorted or partly missing. This pattern tended to tumble due to its incorrect length-to-diameter ratio for the calibre of the gun. A good ratio is between two and a half to three times the diameter or calibre for the length of the projectile. Examples of this particular Selma variety have been recovered from Spanish Fort, Alabama.

Fig. III A-135
Great Britain
Whitworth Pattern I, Sub-pattern I

Fig. III A-136
Great Britain
Whitworth Pattern I, Sub-pattern I

DIAMETER:	1.68 inches across flats, 1.82 inches outer diameter
GUN:	3-pounder Whitworth, 1.7-inch calibre
LENGTH:	5 9/16 inches
WEIGHT:	2 pounds 11 ounces
CONSTRUCTION:	Shell
SABOT:	None
FUZING:	None, brass shipping plug

DIAMETER:	1.69 inches across flats, 1.83 inches outer diameter
GUN:	3-pounder Whitworth, 1.7-inch calibre
LENGTH:	4.69 inches
WEIGHT:	2 pounds 8 ounces
CONSTRUCTION:	Solid shot
SABOT:	None
FUZING:	None

Sir Joseph Whitworth of Manchester, England, patented this Pattern I, Sub-pattern I, projectile on April 23, 1855, Great Britain patent #903. His patent states: "Projectiles [are] made in a spirally shaped form, so as to fit exactly the interior of a piece of ordnance or fire-arm made of a corresponding form, thereby enabling harder metals to be used, economising the force hitherto expended in pressing the projectile into rifle grooves, and diminishing the loss by windage and friction." No battlefield recoveries of the pictured specimen are known to the authors. The use of this Whitworth sub-pattern during the American Civil War is unlikely. Note the untapered base, which was felt to contribute to an unstable flight. The bases in other Whitworth sub-patterns were tapered to correct this defect.

This is a example of an extremely rare calibre Whitworth Pattern I, Sub-pattern I, solid-shot projectile. Whitworth's 3-pounder, 1.7 inch calibre gun weighed 208 pounds. With a charge of eight ounces of powder at an elevation of 35°, it projects its shot with remarkable accuracy to a distance of more than five and a half miles. According to *The Confederate Ordnance Manual,* 1863 edition, the form of the Whitworth projectile was described as a hexagonal prismoid.

Fig. III A-137
Great Britain
Whitworth Pattern I, Sub-pattern II

Fig. III A-138
Great Britain
Whitworth Pattern I, Sub-pattern II

Fig. III A-139
Confederate (copy)
Whitworth Pattern I, Sub-pattern II

DIAMETER:	2.14 inches across flats
GUN:	6-pounder Whitworth rifle, 2.17-inch calibre
LENGTH:	7 1/8 inches
WEIGHT:	5 pounds 14 ounces
CONSTRUCTION:	Solid shot
SABOT:	None
FUZING:	None

Sir Joseph Whitworth patented an improvement on his Whitworth projectile on December 30, 1859, Great Britain patent #2990. His patent states: "The rear part is made to taper, and the weight, form, and degree of convergence given to it must be determined by and adapted to those of the fore part." This improvement gave the Whitworth projectile more favorable accuracy, velocity, and range. The 6-pounder calibre Whitworth projectile was used to a very limited extent; most Whitworths were bolts. The small bursting cavity in the shells made them less effective because of poor fragmentation. This projectile is located in the West Point Military Academy Museum.

DIAMETER:	2.15 inches across flats
GUN:	6-pounder Whitworth rifle, 2.17-inch calibre
LENGTH:	9 inches
WEIGHT:	5 pounds 13 ounces
CONSTRUCTION:	Shell
SABOT:	None
FUZING:	Threaded fuze missing

The 6-pounder (2.17-inch calibre) Whitworth rifle saw very little battlefield use. After the fall of Fort Fisher, North Carolina, on January 15, 1865, four 6-pounder (2.17-inch calibre) Whitworth rifles were surrendered. Whitworth Pattern I, Sub-pattern II, shells in this calibre are extremely rare. The small bursting cavity of the Whitworth pattern made the projectile fragmentation inadequate. Whitworth projectiles were extremely accurate and achieved distances far greater than any other Civil War projectile.

DIAMETER:	2.14 inches across flats
GUN:	6-pounder Whitworth rifle, 2.17-inch calibre
LENGTH:	9 1/16 inches
WEIGHT:	7 pounds 6 ounces
CONSTRUCTION:	Shell
SABOT:	None
FUZING:	CS copper fuze plug, paper time fuze

The Federal Naval Blockade hindered the Confederacy's supply of Whitworth projectiles from Great Britain. This example was an attempt by the Confederates to copy the British-imported Whitworth Pattern I, Sub-pattern II, ammunition, which was often in limited supply. Note the Confederate copper fuze plug and the crude machine marks around the nose of this projectile.

Fig. III A-140
Great Britain
Whitworth Pattern I, Sub-pattern II

DIAMETER:	**2.73 inches across flats**
GUN:	**12-pounder Whitworth rifle, 2.75-inch calibre**
LENGTH:	**9 7/8 inches**
WEIGHT:	**12 pounds 11 ounces**
CONSTRUCTION:	**Solid shot**
SABOT:	**None**
FUZING:	**None**

This is the most common Whitworth bolt pattern recovered. Sir Joseph Whitworth's patent, dated April 23, 1855, Great Britain patent #903, described "projectiles made in a spirally shaped form, so as to fit exactly the interior of a piece of ordnance or fire-arm made of a corresponding form." He patented an improvement dated December 30, 1859, Great Britain patent #2990: "The shape of the fore part depends upon the purpose for which the projectile is to be employed, and may be more or less pointed or curved, or flat fronted. The rear part is made to taper, and the weight, form, and degree of convergence given to it must be determined by and adapted to those of the fore part."

Fig. III A-141
Great Britain
Whitworth Pattern I, Sub-pattern II

DIAMETER:	**2.71 inches across flats**
GUN:	**12-pounder Whitworth rifle, 2.75-inch calibre**
LENGTH:	**9 inches**
WEIGHT:	**8 pounds, 8 ounces**
CONSTRUCTION:	**Shell, case shot**
SABOT:	**None**
FUZING:	**Threaded fuze missing**

This unfired non-battlefield Whitworth shell has a removable nose section that allowed iron segments to be loaded and arranged around the bursting charge. Three pins secured the nose in place. No battlefield recoveries in this Pattern I, Sub-pattern II, variety of Whitworth projectile calibre are known to the authors.

Fig. III A-142
Great Britain
Whitworth Pattern I, Sub-pattern II

DIAMETER:	**2.73 inches across flats**
GUN:	**12-pounder Whitworth rifle, 2.75-inch calibre**
LENGTH:	**10 7/8 inches**
WEIGHT:	**12 pounds**
CONSTRUCTION:	**Shell**
SABOT:	**None**
FUZING:	**Confederate copper fuze plug, paper time fuze**

Note the excellent British workmanship. Although of British origin, this specimen is fitted with a Confederate copper time fuze plug. Both Federal and Confederate forces used the 12-pounder (2.75-inch calibre) Whitworth projectile, although the majority were fired by the Confederates. The 12-pounder (2.75-inch calibre) Whitworth rifle firing a solid-shot projectile with a propellant charge of 1.75 pounds at 35° had a maximum range of 10,000 yards.

Of the effect of Whitworths on Federal troops, Abbot wrote in *Siege Artillery in the Campaigns Against Richmond:* "These projectiles were largely used by the confederates on the lines of Petersburg, where they inspired dread among our men from their long range and horrid sound."

III. Field Artillery Projectiles
A Pictorial Study

B. Non-combat / post-war

The projectiles in this section are considered to be either of non-combat-proven Civil War-era manufacture or of post-war manufacture. The authors—and, indeed, all collectors in the field—would appreciate any substantive proof of actual battlefield use of projectiles shown in this section.

The post-war section is representative and is not meant to be inclusive of all post-war ordnance available. The purpose of this section is to make the student of Civil War artillery aware of those projectiles that could potentially be confused with battlefield-proven Civil War-era ordnance.

The ruins of the arsenal in Richmond, Virginia, in 1865.

Fig. III B-1
Federal
Absterdam Pattern I, Sub-pattern I

Fig. III B-2
Federal
Absterdam Pattern I, Sub-pattern II

Fig. III B-3
Federal
Absterdam Pattern II

DIAMETER:	2.94 inches
GUN:	3-inch rifle
LENGTH:	7 ½ inches
WEIGHT:	8 pounds, 4 ounces
CONSTRUCTION:	Shell
SABOT:	Lead cup
FUZING:	Absterdam (missing)

DIAMETER:	2.94 inches
GUN:	3-inch rifle
LENGTH:	7 1/2 inches
WEIGHT:	8 pounds 2 ounces
CONSTRUCTION:	Shell
SABOT:	Lead cup
FUZING:	Absterdam (missing)

DIAMETER:	2.94 inches
GUN:	3-inch rifle
LENGTH:	8 1/2 inches
WEIGHT:	9 pounds 13 ounces
CONSTRUCTION:	Shell
SABOT:	Brass ring
FUZING:	Absterdam brass fuze plug, paper time fuze

This Absterdam Pattern I, Sub-pattern I, projectile has only one bearing surface. Stamped on the bottom of the lead cup is "PATENTED AUG 12TH 1862"; other specimens have been noted with the stamping "PATENTED S & CO AUGUST 12, 1862." John Absterdam of New York, New York, patented an improvement in banding and covering projectiles on November 7, 1865, patent # 50,783. There are no known battlefield recoveries of this projectile in 3-inch calibre. Some battlefield recoveries of the Absterdam pattern have been noted in the 4.5-inch calibre. Most surviving specimens of this variety are seen with the bearing surface band missing.

This Absterdam Pattern I, Sub-pattern II, projectile has two bearing surfaces, which is less common than the single bearing surface shown in Fig. III B-1. The authors have no knowledge of any 3-inch calibre Absterdam projectiles of this sub-pattern having been recovered from any Civil War battlefield. Most of the surviving examples of this sub-pattern are believed to have originated from the legendary Francis Bannerman's Military Surplus Store. The bottom of the sabot in this specimen is unmarked.

This is the most commonly encountered Absterdam projectile pattern. Most examples are found with the Absterdam fuzes missing. There are no known battlefield recoveries of the Absterdam Pattern II projectiles known to the authors. Stamped into the brass sabot is "ABSTERDAM'S PATENT FEB. 23, 1864." John Absterdam's patent for this projectile was #41,668.

Fig. III B-4
Federal
Delafield

DIAMETER: 3.61 inches
GUN: Delafield banded iron rifle, 3.67-inch calibre
LENGTH: 9 3/16 inches
WEIGHT: 13 pounds 2 ounces
CONSTRUCTION: Shell
SABOT: Malleable cast iron
FUZING: Parrott zinc fuze plug, paper time fuze

This projectile, along with a corresponding rifled cannon, was developed by Lieutenant Colonel Richard Delafield, who was superintendent of the United States Military Academy in West Point, New York, from 1838 to 1845 and again from 1856 to 1861. Delafield referred to this projectile as the "Delafield Malleable Shell." The malleable cast iron base of this projectile has five cast raised flanges that correspond to the Delafield cannon's rifling. A schematic drawing prepared by Delafield of his cannon is dated September 11, 1861. Thirteen of the Delafield banded iron rifles were delivered to the commissary general of the State of New York on March 18, 1862. This specimen is often confused with the Federal 20-pounder Read-Parrott projectile. There have been no known combat finds of the Delafield projectile, and battlefield use is considered unlikely. To the authors' knowledge, the Delafield projectile pattern was not manufactured as a solid shot.

Fig. III B-5
Delafield and Read-Parrott
Comparison views

The 3.67-inch calibre Delafield Malleable Shell is on the reader's left and the 20-pounder (3.67-inch calibre) Read-Parrott projectile is on the reader's right. Note the five distinct flanges on the deeply recessed malleable iron base of the Delafield projectile. The Read-Parrott has five pre-stamped projections in the wrought iron sabot that correspond to the five grooves of the 20-pounder (3.67-inch calibre) Parrott rifle. Another distinguishing characteristic of the Delafield projectile is that it weighs less than the 20-pounder Read-Parrott shell. These two projectiles are often confused with each other until the distinguishing characteristics noted here have been examined.

Fig. III B-6
Federal
Hotchkiss

DIAMETER:	2.94 inches
GUN:	3-inch wrought iron (ordnance) rifle
LENGTH:	6 5/8 inches
WEIGHT:	9 pounds 1 ounce
CONSTRUCTION:	Shell
SABOT:	Lead band
FUZING:	Combination of Hotchkiss percussion and 14-second Hotchkiss-Bormann time fuze

Benjamin B. Hotchkiss patented an improvement for the Hotchkiss projectile on May 16, 1865, patent #47,725. According to the patent, a wooden disk was to be inserted between the base cup and the base of the nose to decrease the risk of premature fracture of the shell during initial firing. The insufficient burning time of the standard-style 5 1/4-second Bormann time fuze for rifled ordnance led to the development of the 14-second Hotchkiss-Bormann version patented on December 24, 1867, patent #72,494. This fuze system was a combination of a modified Hotchkiss percussion fuze and a 14-second Hotchkiss-Bormann time fuze. Note the protective cap that covers the Hotchkiss percussion fuze. The letters "TB" are stamped into the lead band. These letters are often seen in other Hotchkiss specimens of this variety.

Fig. III B-7
Federal
Hotchkiss

DIAMETER:	2.94 inches
GUN:	3-inch wrought iron (ordnance) rifle
LENGTH:	6 5/16 inches
WEIGHT:	8 pounds 14 ounces
CONSTRUCTION:	Shell
SABOT:	Lead band
FUZING:	Combination of Hotchkiss percussion and 14-second Hotchkiss-Bormann time fuze

The base cup on this projectile is flat and therefore of post-war manufacture. The protective cover of the Hotchkiss percussion fuze has been removed to show the flammable material used to help direct flame to the punched 14-second Hotchkiss-Bormann time fuze. If the Hotchkiss-Bormann time fuze failed to ignite or burned beyond the range intended, the center Hotchkiss percussion fuze was designed to detonate the shell on impact. This post-war Hotchkiss variety has been recovered from American Indian War battle sites.

IV. Appendixes

A. Glossary

ARSENAL: The primary place of manufacture and repair for ordnance; this is as opposed to an *armory,* which is the primary place of deposit or storage of same.

BLIND SHELL: A projectile with a hollow cavity which was plugged and therefore not intended to have been fitted with a fuze. The projectile weighed less than a solid shot of the same calibre and thus had increased velocity when fired. The blind shell also decreased the strain on the cannon. It is similar to the cored-shot.

BOLT: Most often an elongated rifled projectile, usually of solid iron, without a cavity or fuze.

BOMBARDMENT: A shower of shells and other incendiary projectiles. Intended to be employed against fortifications, not against open commercial cities, it was nevertheless used at Atlanta, Petersburg, Richmond, and Vicksburg.

BORE DIAMETER: The cannon diameter at the muzzle measured from wall to wall in a smoothbore and from land to land in a rifled tube.

BOURRELET: A French term referring to raised rings that are larger in diameter than the projectile body. These were used as bearing surfaces for the projectile. They were turned on a lathe to the dimension needed so that the projectile would fit into the bore of the cannon. Most often, two bourrelets are located on rifled projectiles and were mainly employed by the Confederates.

BURSTING CHARGE: The charge of gunpowder required for bursting a shell or case-shot. This charge is contained inside the bursting cavity of the projectile.

CALIBRE: The diameter of a cannon's bore expressed in inches, or the weight of the solid shot corresponding to it. The inside diameter of a firing tube (cannon, howitzer, mortar, etc.).

CANISTER: A cylinder made of tin, iron, or sometimes lead, with a removable thin iron top. A heavy iron plate was most often located between the canister balls and the wooden sabot at the bottom. The cylinder contained metal balls, usually made of lead or iron, which were arranged in rows. Commonly sawdust was used to fill the space inbetween these balls. The edges of the vertical cylinder walls were bent over the iron top plate to help keep the canister contents in place. Canister was designed to be used in close range against enemy troops with devastating results.

CARTRIDGE BAG: A cylindrical bag with a circular bottom, made of merino or serge. The material was composed entirely of wool, free from any mixture of thread or cotton, and of sufficiently close texture to prevent the powder from sifting through; that which was twilled was preferred. Flannel was used when the other materials could not be conveniently obtained.

CASE SHOT: Similar to the common shell except that the walls of the projectile are thinner. In both spherical and rifled projectiles, the bursting charge was usually located in a thin metal container, commonly made out of tin or iron. The case-shot material was filled around this container. The internal cavity was usually filled with lead or iron balls in a sulphur or pitch matrix. The small bursting charge of black powder was designed to disperse the case-shot balls in a cone-shaped pattern. The concept was to give the same effects of canister but at much longer ranges. Case shot was invented by an Englishman named Lt. Henry Shrapnel of the Royal Artillery in 1784. See page 10 for a cross-section of a case-shot projectile.

CHILLED IRON: The process by which cast iron was poured into molds, so that the point cooled in contact with a cast iron chill, while the body cooled more slowly in sand. The portion of the cast in contact with the chill develops greater local hardness, crushing strength, and density, but without brittleness in that portion cooled in sand. This method of casting was only applied to rifled solid-shot projectiles. See page 64, figure III A-90, for an example.

COMBINATION FUZE: A fuze that was designed to automatically ignite without needing a flame. If the initial discharge of the cannon did not ignite the fuze, then the fuze was designed to explode on impact.

CONCUSSION FUZE: A fuze that was designed to explode with the projectile in any impact position or angle of impact. Mostly found in spherical projectiles. The Tice Concussion fuze is an example.

CONSTRUCTION: A term used by the authors to describe the interior design of the projectile. Examples are solid shot, common shell, and case-shot.

EARS: This pre-war term originally referred to actual cast-on rings that were located on each side of the mortar's fuze well. By the outbreak of the American Civil War these ear-like rings had been replaced with manufactured indentations, but the use of the term remained. The ears were designed to aid in loading and aligning the projectile so the fuze was in the center of the mortar's bore. Also referred to as tong holes.

FIXED AMMUNITION: Most often a pre-assembled combination of smoothbore projectile, sabot, and powder bag. This assembly allowed for an increase in the rate of fire of the gun crew.

FLAME GROOVES: Grooves cut or cast into the body and/or the sabot of the projectile. These improved the chances of the flame from the firing charge successfully passing over the projectile and lighting the time fuze. See page 55, figure III A-65, for an example.

FLANGE: A projecting rim or ridge on a projectile's body for the purpose of guiding it along the grooves of the cannon, thus imparting rotation. See page 49 for examples.

FUZE: A device screwed or hammer-driven into the body of a projectile. It was designed to ignite the gunpowder bursting charge.

FUZE PLUG: Sometimes called a fuze adapter. A metal or wood device that was screwed or driven into the projectile body to hold a paper time fuze.

HOT SHOT: A solid iron projectile that was intended to be heated red hot. In some cases it was separated from the powder charge by an iron base that acted as a sabot. Its purpose was to create fires in enemy fortifications. It took about 1 1/4 hours to bring cold projectiles to red heat.

LATHE DIMPLE: A drilled or countersunk depression found on the base or sabot of rifled projectiles. This is the true center of the projectile and the site where the lathe arbor held the projectile in place while being turned on a lathe.

LATHE DOG: Found on the ogive or nose of rifled projectiles; often referred to as a lathe lug; a raised area on the body of the projectile that kept it from slipping while being turned to bore tolerance on a lathe.

MALLEABLE CAST IRON: By extracting a portion of the carbon from cast iron, its composition is assimilated to that of wrought iron, thereby increasing the strength; the result is known as malleable cast iron. This type of metal was used to form sabots in certain patterns of projectiles. Upon firing, the pliable iron sabot expanded into the grooves of the cannon without breaking. An example of a malleable cast iron projectile is located on page 86, figure III B-4.

MATRIX: Sulphur, pitch, or rosin added to the interior of a case-shot projectile for the purpose of stabilizing the case-shot balls. This helped to prevent accidental damage to the projectile's bursting charge can or cavity. It also prevented a premature discharge of the bursting charge by movement of the case-shot balls during excessive projectile motion.

NIPPLE: A fitted device attached to the surface contact end of a percussion fuze slider. It was designed to support a percussion cap. Similar to a nipple or cone on a Civil War rifle.

OGIVE: The curve that determines the shape of the nose of a pointed projectile.

ORDNANCE: Comprised of all cannon, howitzers, mortars, cannon-balls, shot, and shells, for land service; all gun carriages, mortar beds, caissons, and traveling forges, with their equipment; and all other apparatus and machines required for the service and maneuvers of artillery in garrisons, at sieges, or in the field; together with the materials for their construction, preservation, and repair.

PAPER TIME FUZES: A tapered, gunpowder-based resin cone wrapped in paper. It was manufactured into standard lengths according to the desired seconds of burn needed. Ignition of the fuze took place at the time of the cannon discharge when the flames traveled past the projectile body to ignite the fuze in the fuze plug.

PATTERN: The initial classification used in describing a particular projectile; primarily based on the date of the patent or, if patent date is unavailable, the evidence of first known field recoveries. In most cases the designations of pattern follow a chronological order of development in that particular style of projectile. Minor variations in the body style, sabot, and fuzing systems do not affect the pattern designation.

PERCUSSION CAP: A cup-like object usually made of copper or brass containing fulminate of mercury. It sat on the nipple end of a fuze slider used with the percussion fuze. On impact, the percussion cap sent a spark to the bursting charge.

PERCUSSION FUZE: A fuze designed to communicate fire to the bursting charge of the projectile at the moment of impact with the ground or other hard surface.

PLUNGER: The inside moveable part of a percussion fuze; sometimes called a striker or slider. Its purpose was to make contact with the percussion cap on the nipple and the anvil cap when the projectile struck a hard surface. This helped direct the discharge flame to the interior black powder charge.

POLYGONAL CAVITY: A method of casting the interior of a spherical common shell which improved the fragmentation. The interior was cast with lines of weakness in various patterns.

POWDER TRAIN: A channel in the interior of the projectile body. Usually a metal tube, the purpose of which was to increase the chances of the detonation charge reaching the bursting charge.

RIFLE: Refers to a cannon tube that was cut with lands and grooves. This was done to improve the accuracy of the rifled projectile.

RIFLING: Often referred to as lands and grooves. A firing tube (cannon) with spiral grooves cut into the bore. The expanding sabot of a fired projectile engaged the grooves for greater accuracy and stability. After groove cutting, those portions of the original smooth bore that remained are called lands and are the actual diameter of the bore.

SABOT: A device made of wood, brass, copper, lead, papier-mâché, leather, rope, or wrought iron. It served as the driving band for the projectile and was forced into the grooves of the rifling of the cannon. This caused rotation that extended the range and improved the stability of the projectile. A wooden sabot was used in a smoothbore cannon to hold the projectile with the fuze forward and in the center of the bore. Often the wooden sabot had one or more grooves on the base to which the cartridge bag was tied.

SEGMENTED SHELL: A concept similar to the polygonal-cavity spherical shell, but used in rifled projectiles. A segmented shell is a projectile that contains small pieces of iron, referred to as segments, which are bonded together to form an interior arrangement around the bursting charge. An example is the Britten projectile located on page 50, figure III A-52.

SERVICE CHARGE: The standard amount of charge of gunpowder based on the weight of the projectile and the bore diameter of the cannon. Also called the propellant charge for the projectile.

SHELL: A hollow projectile filled only with a bursting charge of black powder. Sometimes called the common shell.

SIDE-LOADER: A projectile with a hole in the side of the body other than the fuze opening. This facilitated the insertion of the case-shot material and matrix. It was usually sealed after loading with a lead, iron, brass, or copper threaded plug.

SOLID SHOT: A solid iron projectile without the ability to contain a bursting charge or a fuze. Commonly called a bolt in rifled ordnance. Designed to knock down fortifications or earthworks, or to be fired at lines or columns of troops.

STAND OF GRAPE: Consists of six to nine cast iron balls of a size appropriate to the calibre of the cannon bore. Arranged in two or three tiers of three balls in each tier. Most of the Civil War grapestands were held together by two iron rings and a thick iron plate at each end. A rod in the center was bolted to hold the two plates together. A rope handle fit into two holes in the top iron plate. Some stands known as *quilted grape* were held together by a covering of canvas and a network of twine or wire. Stands of grape were mostly used by naval or seacoast artillery and were rarely used in the field.

SUB-PATTERN: Within a specific projectile pattern there can exist several significant variations in the body, sabot, or fuzing, and/or any combinations of the above. These are commonly referred to as sub-patterns.

TIME FUZE: A fuze designed to explode the projectile a designated number of seconds after the projectile was fired from the cannon or mortar. It was usually fired with a case-shot projectile intended for air burst over troops.

TOW WADS: Rope-like fibers placed in the fuze plug opening to keep debris from entering the projectile's inner cavity. This was packed into the opening with the rounded end of a wooden tool. This material was removed in the field prior to the insertion of the paper time fuze. Tow was also placed between shells to keep them from rattling around and getting damaged in transport.

UNDERPLUG: An iron, brass, or copper circular threaded plug with a hole in its center, smaller than the Bormann fuze. Found in spherical projectiles under the Bormann fuze. This was used to help support the soft metal Bormann fuze from being deformed during firing. See page 10, figure II A-1, for an example.

VARIANT: Within a projectile pattern or sub-pattern there can exist minor differences; such as a wooden drive-in paper time fuze adapter or a threaded paper time fuze adapter.

WINDAGE: Refers to the difference between the bore diameter and the diameter of the projectile.

IV.   Appendixes

B. Bibiliography

*Abbot, Henry L., Brevet General, U.S. Army. *Siege Artillery in the Campaigns Against Richmond*. New York: D. Van Nostrand, 1868.

*Bartleson, John D. *Civil War Explosive Ordnance 1861-1865*. Washington: U.S. Government Printing Office, 1972.

"Description of the Whitworth System of Rifling, Also of Rifled Ordnance and Ammunition." Manchester, N.H: George Falkner, 1867.

*Dickey, Thomas S., and Peter C. George. *Field Artillery Projectiles of the American Civil War*. Atlanta: Arsenal Press, 1980.

Farrow, Edward S. *Farrow's Military Encyclopedia*. New York: published by the author, 1885.

Faust, Patricia L. *Historical Times Illustrated Encyclopedia of the Civil War*. New York:: HarperCollins Publishers, 1986.

*Gibbon, John. *The Artillerist's Manual, Etc*. New York: D. Van Nostrand, 1863.

*Hazlett, James C., Edwin Olmstead, and M. Hume Parks. *Field Artillery Weapons of the Civil War*. Newark, N.J.: University of Delaware Press, 1983.

Hogg, Ian V. *The Illustrated Encyclopedia Of Artillery*. Secaucus, N.J.: Chartwell Books, Inc., 1988.

Jones, J. William. *Southern Historical Society Papers,* Vol. XI. Millwood, N.Y.: Kraus Reprint Company, 1977.

Kerksis, Sydney C., and Thomas S. Dickey. *Field Artillery Projectiles of the Civil War, 1861-1865*. Atlanta: The Phoenix Press, 1968.

Kerksis, Sydney C., and Thomas S. Dickey. *Heavy Artillery Projectiles of the Civil War, 1861-1865*. Atlanta: The Phoenix Press, 1972.

Manigault, Major Edward. *Siege Train: The Journal of a Confederate Artilleryman in the Defense of Charleston*. Columbia, S.C.: University of South Carolina Press, 1986.

*McKee, W. Reid and M.E. Mason, Jr. *Civil War Projectiles II, Small Arms and Field Artillery, With Supplement*. Mechanicsville, Va.: Rapidan Press, 1980.

*Melton, Jr., Jack W., and Lawrence E. Pawl. *Introduction to Field Artillery Ordnance 1861-1865*. Kennesaw, Ga.: Kennesaw Mountain Press, Inc., 1994.

Muzzleloading Artilleryman. Tunbridge, Vt.: Cutter & Locke.

North South Trader's Civil War. Orange, Va.: Publisher's Press, Inc.

*Ripley, Warren. *Artillery and Ammunition of the Civil War*, 4th ed. New York: D. Van Nostrand Reinhold Co., 1984.

Scott, Colonel Henry L. *Military Dictionary*. New York: D. Van Nostrand, 1864.

Spedale, William A. *Historic Treasures of the American Civil War*. Baton Rouge, La.: Land and Land, 1988.

*Thomas, Dean S. *Cannons: An Introduction to Civil War Artillery*. Gettysburg, Pa.: Thomas Publications, 1985.

Wise, Jennings C. *The Long Arm of Lee: The History of the Artillery of the Army of Northern Virginia*. New York: Oxford University Press, 1959.

The War of the Rebellion, 70 volumes bound in 128 parts and a two-part atlas. Washington: U.S. Government Printing Office, 1880-1901.

The Field Manual for the Use of the Officers on Ordnance Duty. Prepared by the Confederate Ordnance Bureau. Richmond, Va.: Ritchie and Dunnavant, 1862.

Recommended readings for artillery projectile enthusiasts are noted with an asterisk (*)

IV. Appendixes

C. Index

A

Abbot, Gen. Henry, U.S.A 17, 33, 48, 76-77, 83
Absterdam, John 85
Absterdam percussion fuze
    pictorial identification 24
Absterdam time fuze
    examples employing 85
    pictorial identification 24
Absterdam projectiles
    examples 85
Alexander, Gen. E.P 61
Archer, Dr. Junius L 41, 44
Archer projectile
    examples 41-47
Armstrong rifle 8, 48
Armstrong projectile
    examples 48
    mention 20, 48
Atlanta Arsenal 69, 71

B

Babcock, G.H 57
Bellona Arsenal 45
Berney, Alfred 15
Blakely projectiles
    examples 49-50
Blakely rifle 8, 49-50, 62, 74, 79
Blind shell
    definition 88
Bolt
    definition 88
Bore diameter
    definition 88
Bormann Braille time fuze
    projectile employing 32
Bormann time fuze
    cross-section 21
    discussion 21, 31-32, 34, 87
    mention 10, 15, 21
    pictorial identification 21, 24, 31, 34
    projectiles employing 10, 15, 20, 31-32, 34, 39, 56, 87
Bourrelet
    definition 88
    example 16
Britten, Bashley 50
Britten percussion fuze

pictorial identification 24
projectiles employing 49-50
Britten time fuze
    pictorial identification 24
Britten projectile
    examples 49-50
    mention 8, 62, 74
Brooke, Cdr. John M., C.S.N. 51
Brooke projectile
    examples 51
    mention 51
Brooke time fuze
    pictorial identification 24
Broun projectile
    examples 52
Broun, William L., C.S.A 52
Bursting charge
    definition 88

C

Calibre
    definition 88
Canister
    cross-section 19
    complete example 19, 35-38
    definition 88
Cartridge bag
    definition 88
Case shot
    cross-section 12-13, 15
    definition 88
Coehorn mortar projectile
    examples 33
Combination fuze
    definition 20, 88
Concussion fuze
    definition 20, 88
    discussion 20
Confederate Bormann time fuze
    cross-section 10
    pictorial identification 10, 24
    projectiles employing 10
Confederate Bormann replacement fuze
    pictorial identification 24
    projectiles employing 31-34
Confederate copy of Bormann time fuze 21, 31-34
Confederate copies of Federal projectiles

examples 58, 76, 68, 82
Confederate copper time fuze plug
    cross-section 10, 16
Confederate percussion fuze
    projectiles employing 73
Confederate West Point percussion fuze
    pictorial identification 24
    projectiles employing 57
Copper fuze plug
    projectiles employing 16, 24, 34, 48, 51,
                                          61-62, 69-74, 76, 82-83

D

Delafield, Col. Richard 86
Delafield projectile
    examples 86
Delafield and Parrott:
    a comparison 86
Delafield rifle 86
Dyer, Alexander B 37, 53
Dyer projectile
    examples 12, 53
    mention 9, 37

E

Eagle Machine Works 69
Ears
    definition 88

F

Fixed ammunition
    definition 88-89
Flame grooves
    definition 89
Flange
    definition 89
Forrest's Artillery 51
Fuze
    definition 89
Fuze plug
    definition 89

G

Gibbon, John 29

Grapeshot
    see *Stand of grape*

H

Holcomb's Vermont Battery 75
Hot shot
    definition 89
Hotchkiss, Andrew 54, 57
Hotchkiss, Benjamin 55-57, 87
Hotchkiss combination fuze
    projectiles employing 56, 87
Hotchkiss percussion fuze
    cross-section 13
    pictorial identification 24
    projectiles employing 13, 20, 55, 57, 87
Hotchkiss projectile
    cross-section 13
    examples 36, 54-57, 87
    mention 9
Hotchkiss time fuze plug, brass
    discussion 20, 23, 55, 56
    pictorial identification 13, 23-24
    projectiles employing 13, 55-57

I

Iron anvil cap (West Point type) percussion fuze
    projectiles employing 57, 65

J

James, Charles T 14, 39, 59, 60
James percussion fuze
    cross-section 14
    pictorial identification 24
    projectiles employing 14, 20, 59-60
James projectile
    cross-section 14
    examples 14, 38-39, 58-60
    mention 28, 57
James rifle 38, 57, 59-60

L

Lathe dimple
    definition 89
Lathe dog
    definition 89

Lead fuze plug
    projectile employing 55
Leading of the bore 60
Loading ears 33

M

Matrix
    definition 89
Mullane (Tennessee-sabot) projectiles
    examples 61-62

N

Napoleon cannon 8, 29
Nipple
    definition 89

O

Ogive
    definition 89
Ordnance rifle (wrought iron rifle) 8, 36, 53-56,
    62, 67, 72, 76, 87

P

Paper time fuze
    definition 20, 23, 28, 89
    pictorial identification 24
    projectiles employing 10-13, 15-16, 23, 30, 33-34,
    44-48, 51-53, 55-57, 61-62, 65-66,
    68-74, 76, 78-79, 82-83, 85-86

R

Read, Dr. John B. 8, 61, 68
Read projectile
    cross-section 16
    examples 16, 67, 70, 72-73
    mention 8, 9, 61, 63
Read vs. Parrott:
    discussions 8, 16, 63, 68
    examples 15, 63-65, 68-71, 74, 86
Richmond Arsenal 52
    picture 84
Rifle
    definition 90
Rifling
    definition 90

S

Sabot
    definition 90
Sawyer, Addison M 36-37, 75
Sawyer combination fuze
    pictorial identification 24
    projectile employing 75
Sawyer percussion fuze
    pictorial identification 24
    projectile employing 75
Sawyer projectile
    examples 37, 75
    mention 20
Sawyer rifle 37, 75
Sawyer, Sylvanus 75
Schenkl combination fuze
    discussion 22
    pictorial identification 22
    projectiles employing 17, 76
Schenkl, John P 77
Schenkl percussion fuze
    cross-section 17, 22
    pictorial identification 24
    projectiles employing 17, 53, 76-77
Schenkl projectiles
    cross-section 17
    examples 17, 76, 78
    mention 9, 20, 60
Segmented shell
    definition 90
Sellers (William) & Co 53
Selma Arsenal 30, 41, 44, 52, 73, 79-80
Selma Arsenal "G" mark 30, 80
Selma projectile
    examples 30, 41, 44, 52, 73, 79-80
Shell
    definition 90
Side-loader
    definition 90
Smith, C.W 57
Solid shot
    definition 90
Stand of grape
    definition 40, 90
    examples 40
Stetson, T.D 59

T

Taylor time fuze
    pictorial identification 24
Tennessee sabot
    see *Mullane*
Time fuze
    definition 20, 90
    discussion 20, 22, 23
Tredegar Iron Works 8, 16, 69

U

Underplug
    definition 90

W

Washington Arsenal 68

Washington Artillery 46
West Point 40, 46, 48, 57, 64, 72, 82, 86
Whitworth rifle 81-83
Whitworth projectile
    examples 81-83
Whitworth, Sir Joseph 81-83
Windage
    definition 90
Wooden fuze plug
    cross-section 11
    pictorial identification 24
    projectiles employing 11, 30, 33, 44-45, 47,
        51-52, 61-63, 68-69, 71-72, 74, 78-79

Z

Zinc fuze plug
    projectiles employing 12, 15, 53, 57, 63, 65-66, 86

Steven's Knoll, and East Cemetery Hill in the background, Gettysburg, PA.

About the authors

Jack W. Melton, Jr.

Jack W. Melton, Jr., a life-long resident of Georgia, was born in Columbus on May 10, 1960. Both geography and heredity destined him to be a student of the Civil War: he grew up adjacent to the Kennesaw Mountain National Military Park near Kolb Farm, and several of his ancestors fought for the South during the war. His mother's grandfather, Jeff Love, was an artillery driver for Milton's Light Artillery, and his father's great-grandfather, Samuel Troup Carter, was in the 14th Alabama Infantry. Both of his parents are collectors of Civil War artifacts.

His interest in the history-rich area surrounding him spurred him to respond to the National Park Service's need for a historical trail through their Kennesaw Mountain National Battlefield Park. This work became his Eagle Scout project, and he became a Bicentennial Eagle Scout on Independence Day 1976. Since that time, thousands of people have walked the trail he cut at Kennesaw Mountain.

He began relic hunting at age 14, and found his first 12-pounder solid shot that same year while hunting with his dad. Thus began his interest in the field artillery projectiles of the War Between the States. In the ensuing years, his interest in excavated artillery projectiles has taken him from Port Hudson to Gettysburg, and he has recovered nearly 250 projectiles.

Deeply affected by the death of renowned artillery collector and author Thomas Dickey, Sr., in 1987, Jack was moved to continue the work of the man he so admired, researching, photographing, and studying the wide variety of projectiles and their patents.

He entered the realm of professional Civil War dealers when he purchased a collection in 1988. He discovered that he had an affinity for buying and selling artifacts, and he opened his first shop in 1989. He also began to pursue professional photography, and his work has appeared in a number of national publications. He is a featured front cover photographer for *North South Trader's Civil War* magazine.

Today he owns and operates Kennesaw Mountain Military Antiques in Kennesaw, Georgia. He also completed the professional photography program at the Southeastern Center for the Arts in Atlanta and graduated with honors. He was selected as an Honored Member in the National Directory of Who's Who in Executives and Professionals, 1994-1995.

Lawrence E. Pawl

Lawrence E. Pawl was born December 6, 1948, in Grand Rapids, Michigan. He completed his undergraduate work at Michigan's Grand Valley State University and was graduated with a degree in Health Sciences. He went on to obtain his medical degree at Wayne State Medical School in Detroit. His interest in the Civil War dates back to age 14, when he attended a Civil War show in Detroit. He purchased his first artillery shell at age 25—a 3.67-inch Hotchkiss fired at Shiloh—and his fascination with the projectiles of the Civil War was born.

In the late 1970s, he encountered two books that were to have a profound effect on him. In an it's-a-small-world coincidence, Grand Rapids medical colleague Jack O'Donnell introduced him to *The Illustrated History of American Civil War Relics,* written by O'Donnell's brother Mike and Stephen W. Sylvia. He then encountered a copy of Dickey and George's *Field Artillery Projectiles of the American Civil War* and began to correspond with and purchase projectiles from Tom Dickey. He recalls that Tom often shipped the weighty shells cross-country to him via Greyhound bus.

A mutual interest in artillery projectiles brought together co-authors Pawl and Melton in the mid-1980s. This volume is the result of their shared love of research on the surviving projectiles and their patents.

Dr. Pawl has been in private practice in Grand Rapids since 1981, specializing in medical oncology. In his leisure hours, of which there aren't nearly enough, he also collects excavated Civil War weaponry, including swords, longarms, and handguns. His collecting interests also go as far afield as astronaut memorabilia, particularly items relating to Apollo 11 and Buzz Aldrin.

He has two teenage children: son Andy (who, much to his father's delight, is showing some interest in the War Between the States) and daughter Sarah.

Top: co-authors Jack W. Melton, Jr., and Lawrence E. Pawl at the United States Military Academy at West Point, New York. Photo by Andrew Pawl.